Islan
Theory and Practice in Education

By

Elsayed Soleit

Content

INTRODUCTION

CHAPTER I

INTRODUCTION

- Islamic System of Education
- Need and Significance
- Statement of the Problem
- Definition of Terms
- Aims and Objectives
- Scope of the Study
- Delimitation
- Hypotheses

INTRODUCTION

Education enables man to live in the contemporary society successfully by giving him systematic intellectual and moral instruction and training. His knowledge, abilities, character, mental faculties etc. are developed through a well-planned process of education.

Unprecedented changes have taken place in all areas of modern education, especially in terms of restatement of its aims, restructuring of its curricula, re-scheduling of teaching-learning processes, re-consideration of the socio-economic status of the teacher, re-definition of the value system etc. Modern treatises on education depict this changing trends. For a long time, the shaping and development of character of the child was considered one of the chief objectives of education. Now-a-days its aim has been re-stated in economic terms as the investment in human resource development which, of course, includes the development of character and inculcation of permanent values in individuals. This tendency in education is indicative of the continuous growth of education as a science.

Very often in the present context, the word 'modern' implies the Western system of education of modern times. The whole exercise of education revolves round the processes of learning and teaching which have undergone a continuous evolution.

Understanding the nature of the child and the society in which the activity of education takes place, is the first requisite of a teaching – learning programme. Educational objectives are based on the philosophy of life of a particular society in which educational exercise is going on. The curriculum content is selected according to the needs of the children on the one hand and the needs of the society on the other. All educational systems are rooted in the past and are compounds of a variety of constituent factors influencing educational institutions and their functions. The political development of a country is another potent factor that influences the educational system. Nations committed to a particular ideology apply their beliefs to their systems of education. Many Western nations have accepted the secularization as a principle of their educational systems. Any country in the world moulds its educational policies according to the views of its educational and political philosophers.

It is an accepted fact that as society changes, the system of education also positively responds to it. The philosophy of life that the society upholds naturally gives character and colour to the system of education also. But at the same time, a powerful system of education strongly interacts with the social philosophy and structure of the society and brings about social change. Therefore change is the very hallmark of an effective system of education.

Philosophy of education has changed itself by passing through different ages. It has brought about both theoretical and practical changes in the system of education from time to time. This has affected not only the aims and objectives of education, but the techniques of curriculum transaction and organizational aspects also. A glimpse of the history of education through ages would reveal this fact.

The education during the middle ages in Europe, as everybody knows, was not very much democratic, life-oriented or vocationalized. Its chief objective was the preservation of knowledge and dissemination of certain acceptable ideas. The educational scenes were dominated by the private interests of a particular upper strata of society. The condition of Europeans during the 'dark ages' is self explanatory from its history. The surprising differences in the characteristic features of the education of modern time from that of the 'dark ages' are perhaps the results of inescapable influences exerted by certain factors of the Western system of education.

Modern education, therefore can be considered as the sum total of various strains of thoughts which it has assimilated into its system from time to time. Different cultural outlooks and views on life, techniques etc. have influenced the Western system of education. Islam of course, is one of them. The present study aims at examining the influences that the Islamic philosophy exerted on modern system of education.

The very philosophy of education of the modern nations that education is a powerful instrument for bringing about economic and technological development, was very well known to the Islamic scholars from its very inception. 'Value education, about which the modern – societies speak profusely in the present context of erosion of permanent values which has become a menace to the formation of modern society, was one of the basic tenets of Islamic system of education throughout its history. This is equally applicable to the democratic values of equality, liberty, fraternity and empowerment of the lower strata of the society etc. about the necessity of which there is an abundance of literature now-a-days.

Islamic system of Education

Islam is a religion which has spread across the diverse cultures of the world. The Islamic culture and civilization emerged and influenced various societies of Asia, Africa and Europe. The intellectual culture of the Muslim world remained intact. The first centre of the Islamic education and Muslim culture was Madina in Saudi Arabia, the second was Damscus in Syria and the third one was Baghdad in Iraq. Many renowned Muslim personalities flourished during the Middle ages. They made unique and influential contributions to different branches of knowledge such as medicine, philosophy, geography, astronomy, mathematics, sociology etc. At present its influence extends to millions of people in the continents of America, Asia and Australia. Ibn Khaldun, Imam al-Ghazali, Ibn Rushd, Ibn Sina, Al-Kindi etc. were some of the most famous thinkers and philosophers of the period. History has recorded that the Abbasid period of Muslim rule in Spain was a land-mark in the progress of science and education. Cordova University of Muslim Spain was the world famous centre for education, research and culture.

During the 'Dark Ages' in Europe, the spread of Islamic knowledge, ideas and philosophy revitalized the European system of education. No student of history of education can forget the cardinal role that the centres of Islamic learning played in the preservation and dissemination of knowledge and culture in Europe. The confluence of scholarship and interaction of the scholars helped Europe to build up a new philosophy of life which naturally influenced its system of education also. There are living evidences in the annals of education and philosophy in proof of this.

The Arab Muslims built both an empire and a culture of their own. No people in the 'Middle ages' contributed to human progress so much as did the Arabs and the Arabic speaking people. Arabic was the language of learning and culture and progressive thought throughout the civilized world, for many centuries. The Arabic literature was placed at its highest peak at this time. The 'Seven Odes' of Tharafat and six other poets, the masterpieces of poetical compositions, was the world famous poetry series in that period. The unique contributions of scholars like Al-Ghazzali, Ibn-Khaldun, Ibn Rushd, Al-kindi, Al-Farabi and Al-Razi to the field of education, science, philosophy are still unmatched.

Islamic education has its own peculiar character, which distinguishes it very clearly from all other types of educational theory and practice. This distinguishing factor is due to the ambient presence and influence of Holy Qur'an on Islamic education. Islam lifts man from the concrete to the abstract and from the actual to the ideal.

Islam has abolished all kinds of discriminations whatever be their bases. All types of genetic, ethnic and nationalistic discriminations were declared inadmissible by Islam. And racial, social or cultural discrimination which exists even today in the so-called countries, was declared unlawful by Islam. To understand this one needs to go through Prophet's farewell speech only. The culture of Islam, which is living and self-renovating one is itself on par with the highest and most advanced contemporary cultures of the world.

Islamic education always insisted on the unity of knowledge and unity of mankind. It is a system based on man's faith in God, and his unconditioned submission to Him. Eternal values emerge from such a deep faith. Islamic education has always an uncompromising attitude towards insistence on human and social values.

Need and Significance

Muslim population all over the world, especially in India is reported to be very backward in educational achievements. It can be even stated that there is a negative motivational factor which keeps majority of

Muslims away from modern education. This is partially because of the wide-spread conservative feeling against modern education that it is not in agreement with Islamic philosophy. Though eminent Indians like Sir Syed Ahmed Khan, Maulana Abul Kalam Azad, Dr. Zakir Husain etc. worked hard to dispel this misbelief, the apathy towards Western education still lingers among the Muslims of India. The situation being this, it is felt that it is the duty of an educated Muslim to bring out the fact that modern system of education and its theory and practice are not antithetical to the Islamic philosophy and, is in fact, Islamic strains of thought and views on life and man, have directly or indirectly influenced the existing system of education. It is also strongly felt that any attempt to bring out the features of inter-relatedness between the Islamic and modern philosophies of education would help to instil confidence in the Muslim population and enthuse them to pursue modern education.

The contribution of Islamic philosophy to modern education is not widely recognized by the educationists and it has been neglected to a certain extent, especially by most of the Western educational thinkers. There are several papers and treatises dealing with the various aspects of the subject presented by them with the result that they have generated so many misconceptions about the aim, content and role of Islamic education. The compartmentalization of religious and Secular education based on the fictitious division of life into spiritual and temporal is not approved by Islam. The epithet 'Islamic education' becomes absurd if it does not agree with the totality of life. And there exists a view that Muslim education is simply religious and aimed at producing religiousmen who had conservative views on contemporary problems of life. Probably it was because of this out-dated education that Muslim society of the later Middle Ages became backward. The present study aims to bring about a better understanding of the Islamic philosophy and its influence on modern education in the right perspective by comparing mainly the views of Imam Ghazzali (AD 1058-1111), Ibn Rushd (1126-1198) and Ibn Khaldun (1332-1406) on educational theory and practice with those of modern Western educationists like Comenius (1592-1670), Rousseau (1712-1778) and John Dewey (1859-1952) etc. with a view to examining the influence of the former on the later.

A study which traces the influence of Islamic philosophy on Western educational thoughts and practice as far as the investigator is aware of, doesn't exist. If at all there is one it is more or less influenced of Arabic literature and Islamic scholars. Being a student of Education, Islamic history and Arabic language and literature, the investigator felt interested in studying the influence of Islamic teachings on Western schools of thought, especially those of education. Since this work is of a combination of historical and analytical nature, the investigator expects that the study will stimulate the thoughts of all those who are interested in education.

Statement of the Problem

The present study therefore is entitled 'The influence of Islamic Philosophy on the theory and Practice of Education'.

Definition of Terms

Islamic Philosophy: Islamic philosophy in this thesis means the philosophy of Islam based on the Holy Qur'an and Hadith or the Traditions of Prophet Muhammed as interpreted and explained by authentic Islamic scholars. This philosophy is reflected in the Islamic views on life, nature of man, his place in the world, value system, society etc.

Education: Education means modern systems of education which emerged and developed as a result of the thoughts of the modern educational philosophers like Comenius, Rousseau and John Dewey etc.

Aims and Objectives of the Study

1. To understand the main characteristic features of Islamic philosophy.
2. To understand the general features of Islamic philosophy of education in terms of :
   a) Aims and Objectives
   b) Curriculum Development
   c) Curriculum Transaction
   d) Teacher Pupil Interaction
   e) Educational Management

3. To make a comparative examination of the educational theories and practices enunciated by Islamic philosophers represented by Imam Ghazzali, Ibn Rushd and Ibn Khaldun and Western philosophers represented by Comenius, Rousseau and John Dewey with a view to ascertaining the influence of the former on the later.

4. To assess the nature of the influence of Islamic philosophy on the modern education in terms of:

    a) Aims and Objectives
    b) Curriculum Development
    c) Curriculum Transaction
    d) Teacher Pupil Interaction
    e) Educational Management

Hypotheses

i. Islam has an independent philosophy which can be interpreted in terms of (a) nature of man and his place in the world (b) nature of knowledge and (c) nature of values.

ii. There exists a system of education evolved from Islamic philosophy and it can be identified and described in terms of its characteristics related to:

    a) Aims and Objectives
    b) Curriculum development
    c) Curriculum transaction
    d) Teacher pupil interaction
    e) Educational management

iii. Islamic philosophy has directly or indirectly influenced the theory and practice of modern education and this influence can be identified and described in terms of its features related to:

a) Aims and Objectives

b) Curriculum development

c) Curriculum transaction

d) Teacher pupil interaction

e) Educational management

iv. It is possible to identify the direct or indirect influence of Islamic philosophy on modern theories and practice of education by comparing the select representative philosophers like Imam Ghazzali, Ibn Khaldun and Ibn Rushd with Comenius, Rousseau and John Dewey.

Scope of the Study

Islam, one of the largest religions of the world, has a philosophy with certain unique characteristic features which distinguish it from other philosophies and schools of thought. One of these features is that its philosophical views remain basically constant and true, despite the drastic changes occurring in the world due to scientific and technological innovations and transformations. This is indicative of its permanent nature. Though the Western philosophy of education has changed from time to time since Renaissance, Islam's views on education remained the same. Though this trend of Islamic philosophy can be interpreted as conservatism, the reality is that it remains as a moderate eclectic philosophy which has influenced the other systems of thought. The present study, it is hoped, would establish this fact. Besides, it is also contemplated that once it is brought out that the Islamic philosophy has influenced the modern philosophies of education, the apathetic attitude of the conservative Muslims towards modern education, to a certain extent, could be dispelled

Delimitation

The main purpose of the study is to carry out an analytical study of the various aspects of the Islamic philosophy of education and their influence, if any, on modern system of education. This being a wide area from the point of view of both theory and practice of education, the investigator has confined his attempts to identify the influence in certain areas of education such as: aims and objectives, curriculum, methods of teaching and learning, educational organization and management etc.

Hence the study will be confined to examining the traces of direct or indirect influence of Islamic philosophy on the theory and practice of education in modern times in the following areas only:

1. Aims and Objectives
2. Curriculum development
3. Curriculum Transaction

4. Teacher-pupil Interaction
5. The organization and management of education

Besides, the study will be confined to the examination of relevant similarities of philosophical strains in the educational thoughts of Islamic and Western Philosophers and their bearing on the theory and practice of education.

REVIEW OF RELATED LITERATURE

K. Abdul Waheedu "Influence of islamic philosophy on the theory and practice of education " Thesis. Department of Educaton, University of Calicut, 2003

CHAPTER II

REVIEW OF RELATED LITERATURE

REVIEW OF RELATED LITERATURE

Examination of related literature is a highly essential aspect of any educational research. As far as the research in the Islamic education is concerned, there has been scarcely any research which is directly related to the present type of study. However, there are several books and papers on the Islamic philosophy in general and Islamic educational philosophy in particular. The articles on the various aspects of Islamic education (especially based on Quran) are also available for reference. Therefore, in the following paragraphs, an attempt has been made to give a brief account of relevant literature and studies which are directly or indirectly related to the areas of the present study.

T.B. Irving (1976) examines, 'Muslim Contribution to Western Culture' and examines the contribution made to the World Civilization, especially to knowledge, science and education by the Muslims. He says: "Islamic world had a unique outlook on life or it contemplated the oneness of the Divinity and thus taught the world to appreciate culture when Romans had passed away and lost the direction of the society". "The concern for learning had already flowered through the great Islamic universities' centres of study into western Europe. This eventually brought the rebirth of intellectual activity and freedom which was called that world's renaissance. Contemporary science is based on its foundation".

Dr. Ilyas Ba Unus (1977), who is a professor of sociology at the State University of New York stresses the need for education for social cohesion. He examines the 'Principles of Ideological Education'.

In this paper he distinguishes three types of education- Pragmatic education, regenerated education and ideological education, and explains the details of the third one ie., ideological education. He says "by ideology I mean a system of values which govern and interrelates the totality of the societal life- political, economic recreational and all other forms of interpersonal relation that exists in society". He emphasizes that Islamic education is based on the ideology as defined by him and it has contributed his idea to the world. He enumerates ten basic principles reflected in such a system of education.

Prof. Muhammad Al Mubarak (1977) presented a paper on 'The Islamic System of Education'. He examines the past, present and future of the Islamic system of education with a view to highlighting its glory in the past and conveying its message to the future generation of educationists. He says "this generation must, however, be qualified by the admission that their existed in every Muslim country, even in the darkest periods, outstanding scholars with creative minds". About the position of teachers he says "the teachers commanded great prestige so much so that kings and governors used to hold them in high esteem.

Ahamed Khizar Zuberi (1977), presented a paper on 'The Concept of God among Children'. In this research report Ahamed Khizar Zuberi explains his attempts to derive the underlying principles of the formation of the concept of God by children; This research is based on the data already gathered by Piaget for the examination of the concept formation by the children, and Mr. Zuberi re-examines certain conclusion made by Piaget from the data, and reinterprets them. Hence he adopts a novel method of research by reinterpreting the data used by the world renowned developmental psychologists and comes to the conclusion that the children have a tendency to form the concept of God as enunciated in the Holy Qura'n. In this paper Mr. Zuberi uses a few technical terms used by Piaget with the same meaning. Examples are animism, diffuse artificialism, artificialism, immanent artificialism, internal aritificialism, assimilation, accommodation, etc. The following statements of the author indicates his conclusion.

"It is possible to interpret the data collected by Piaget which does not necessarily involve the permanent conflict within the child as a child believes that all objects have been manufactured by a manufacturer for the child's personal benefits, he has motion or at least a nucleus of a motion of God who is the creator and benevolent provider'. This notion may be very vague and rudimentary, but still a child, at least has the potentiality to conceive of God in all His majesty and bounty."

"It is interesting to note that some elements of the child's spontaneous and liberated convictions are the basic elements of the teaching of Islam".

In conclusion the author says that 'the basic fact is that a child learning about God as the Creator and Designer of the Universe by acting and contemplating on the Creatures'. "The child also develops the concept of God by acting on the physical and social environment".

Dr. Shaikh Muhammed Iqbal (1978) presents the summary of his paper, 'An Islamic Concept of Education', presented at International Muslim Seminar held in Sri Lanka in July 1978. In this paper he examines the Islamic concepts of education in the modern context. He remarks "the present pattern of education is without true goal. Its aim is either to produce clerks, technicians, researcher in fine arts or the bulk of job hunters". The basic objective of education should be to build the forces of human unity, to modernize the country, and to impart education in socio-moral values. "The Islamic pattern of education in its heyday fulfilled the demand and result were encouraging. It was liberal without loosing the fundamental objective of making human being responsible in their relationships and actions". He suggests: education in Islam does not ignore the practical side of human life. The aimlessness and impracticability of the curricula and the challenge of student unrest can be met halfway by linking the present with the brilliant past and by opening vocational and professional institutions. The early Muslims had never downgraded practical training in education.

Sayyid Sadiq al-Mahdi (1978) has presented the summary of a paper 'The Influence of Islamic Thought on Europe' in a symposium organized by the Islamic University of Omdurman. The period he selects for the study is between the middle of the 7th Century to the middle of the 17th Century AD. He divides the paper into four sections, and examines the force of Islam which established the Universal Islamic State, and created the Islamic culture, the impact Islam exercise in Europe, the different attitudes of Europe to the Islamic impact and the fraternal relations between people.

He explains that many important ideas which were originally conceived and discussed by Muslim thinkers appeared as new ideas in European thought centuries later. For examples he says that through Ibn Khaldun was the first author who elected and explained sociological ideas.

Syed Muhammed al-Naquib (1979) conducted a study on 'Aims and Objectives of Islamic Education'. In the study he states that education preserves and transmits the basic values of a society, the central aims of education is the balanced growth of human personality. In his view, the aim of Islamic education is the creation of good and righteous man who builds up the structure of his earthly life according to the 'Shariah' and employs it to subserve his faith. Worship in Islam is both extensive and comprehensive; it is not restricted to the physical performance of religious rituals only but it embraces all aspects of activity, faith, thought, feeling and work. Two things must be achieved through education: (i) it must enable man to understand his Creator in the true sense (ii) it must enable him to understand the ways of Allah in the Universe, explore the earth and re-inforce his religion. He declares that the sources of knowledge pertain to two categories: (i) Divine revelation (ii) The human intellect, its constant interaction with the universe by observation, contemplation, experimentation and application. Man cannot, by himself, be rightly guided to the Divine truth and life cannot be regulated in the proper manner, hence the need of Divine revelation. According to Islamic view, man is considered the Vicegerent of God on earth. God has given man authority in actual life. Man must acquire wisdom which transforms him into a good man and a wise master. Islam presents a universal and rationally acceptable norm in the concept of Man and God. The concept of one God, one humanity and one religion from the days of Adam; the norm of human values is the service for all humanity in all ages. It saves man from being proud and teacher him humility by creating in him the feeling that all power of man is delegated to him by God. It is not his own. This concept leads man to a better understanding of others and to peace and happiness among nations and races. Man is to consider this life not as an end itself but as a means and process to lead a complete and better life in the hereafter. This concept of faith and action accordingly, will lead to the betterment of man and society, a methodology of self analysis and criticism, and it will generate actually sensible individuals fully aware of rights, duties and responsibilities and thoroughly conscious of their own short comings.

Love of God and the Prophet are the major means of acquiring this sensitivity which includes both intellectual awareness and innate response. The aim of education in Islam is to produce a good man.

Justice M.M.Abdul Cader (1980), former Judge of Court of Appeals, Sri Lanka has attempted an analysis of the essential features of Islamic Education by citing evidences from authentic books. He has stated, "We forget that Iman (belief) and Islam (practice) together constitute a true Muslim. The test of faith is the practice thereof". He concluded saying that total commitment to Islam must commence at home, continue with learning at school; Islam is said to be a religion of reason. He has enumerated essential features of Islamic education in this paper.

Prof.Abdul Kadar Hubaiti (1981) explained the basic Islamic concepts of education in his authentic essay published in the journal, 'Muslim World League'. He has reported that there are 750 Verses in the Qur'an about education, learning and knowledge, whereas the Verses devoted to matters of worship such as prayer, fasting, zakat, charity and the like are no more than 150. By citing quotations from Qur'an he highlights the emphasis given by Islam for the acquisition of knowledge. He has enumerated 11 basic principles of Islamic education.

He concluded saying "If we consider the Qur'anic concepts from the view point of modern education, they will be readily and unanimously accepted and admired by all modern educationists and thinkers. Infact, these concepts are highly advanced. Modern education falls short of implementing many of these profound educational concepts.

Dr. A. Rahman(1981) studied on 'The Qur'anic Education-Problems and Prospects'. In this article Dr. Rahman examines the basic principles of Qur'anic education and foes on tracing the history of early Islamic schools. He comes to a genaralisation that "in spite of a slight variance in the course content in various countries, the general syllabi' of the Islamic schools remained same". In the light of the principles of Quranic education and the generalisation derived from history he examines how the Islamic principles of education influenced education in Nigeria. He traces the influences of Islam in Nigeria for 8th century AD onwards.

Dr. Muhammed Muslehuddin (1985) conducted comparative study of Islamic Legal System Philosophy of Islamic Law and the Orientalists. He has divided the area as five parts and 26 chapters.

He discussed in Part one the Main Branches of Philosophy' as Metaphysic and Epistemology or Theory of Knowledge. In this chapter he has discussed the philosophers like Descartes, Socrates, John Locke, Hume, Kant etc. And then explained on different aspects of law like, the law itself, schools of law, Benthan's Philosophy and Greek Philosophers etc; in the 2nd part. Then he explained Historical Background of Natural

Laws like 'Law of Fairness, Justice, Human Reason and Stoic Philosopher. Then he narrated the factors of destruction of natural law. Positivism in Law was discussed in detail.

In the third part, he made a clear picture of Islamic Law. The Laws prevailed in the Pre-Islamic Ages to the laws in the present Muslim States. He explained 'Justice', 'Order and Peace' Reason & Revelation etc. Then he stressed the need of ijitihad (Interpretation). Then the different aspects of Analogy (Quiyas) and Ijma'(consensus) and other sources of law are described in detail.

The part IV of the study is fitted as 'Orientalists and Recent Publications'. The views of the orientalists have been discussed in the topics: Revelation and reason, Unity and Diversity, Idealism and Realism, Law and Morality etc. In part five, the Islamic Legal System of the world is given. The family law of Islamic System and the social law have been discussed and compared with that of the laws prevalent in the world today. Also the Islamic law is compared with the ancient laws like 'Roman Law' etc.

'In Islam, law and religion, law and morals, law and the so-called 'church' are inseparable. It has absolute students of justice as they are based upon the norms of vice and virtue which are supported by revelation and the fundamental principles of law. This is the distinctive feature of Islamic justice. The Qur'an was responsible for great discussions and to it was indirectly due to marvelous development of all branches of science in the Muslim world.

Mohammed Sharifkhan (1986) has studied the various aspects of 'Islamic Education'. The place of education in Islam has been dealt with in detail in this study. Historical development, curriculum, teacher pupil relationship, old schools of Islamic learning, the characteristics of medieval Islamic learning, significance of Fiqh, role of Madrasas, education for preparation to life, contribution of Muslim learning to world civilization and place of vocational education in Islamic learning etc. have been discussed in the study. The author also discussed the aims and objectives of Islamic education, objectives of Islamic curriculum, special educational problems of Indian Muslims, modernization of Islamic education, spread of Muslim culture to other civilizations, historical development of higher education, concept of education, practical life and moral values in Islamic education etc. He has again written about the philosophical views on education of Imam Al Ghazzali; methods and techniques of teaching, physical and health education and psychological views etc.

Dr. M. Ziauddin Alavi (1988) conducted a study on 'Muslim Educational thought in the Middle Ages'. Dr. Alavi presented a treatise on Muslim Educational thought in the Middle Ages. It is an exhaustive study on the Islamic contribution to education in the Middle Ages, alongwith historical background of the development of education.

In the present work, it is dealt with the philosophical concepts of the Holy Quran and the terms like Reality, Knowledge, Worship of God etc. which have been discussed from their philosophical perspective. The Muslim educational thought has been analysed in the light of different schools of philosophy. The philosophy of Plato, Aristotle and other philosophers has also been touched with the objective to trace the extent of their influence over Arab Philosophers. An attempt has been made to trace the development of Muslim Education from the rise of Islam upto 14th century in its philosophical, religious and political setting. In addition to this, an attempt has been made to examine critically the contributions of Muslim Scholars to education like Ibn Sina, Al-Ghazzali and Ibn Khaldun, Ibn Rushd etc. These eminent Muslim philosophers have made valuable contributions to the promotion of Muslim education and Islamic jurisprudence. The concepts and ideas evolved by them have been critically examined with their impact upon the Muslim education in the Islamic civilization.

An attempt has also been made to assess the influence of Muslim philosophers and educators on Western educational thought and on revival of learning in Europe and the Establishment of Universities. This is followed by a critical examination of the education system of the Muslims as well as to dispelling some misconceptions about the education system. The author has given a brief account of the aim, contents, methodology of teaching and organization of the Muslim education. The course of study, methods of teaching and status of a teacher are most important components of every system of education. The author has made an in-depth study of all these concepts in a lucid manner. Lastly, the relevance of the Muslim educational thought for the Muslims of today has been discussed. An attempt has been made to trace the development of Islamic education system from the rise of Islam upto the 14th century in its philosophical and religious setting and to examine critically the contribution of the Muslim scholars and philosophers to education in all its varied aspects. This study aims a better understanding of the Muslims' education as a whole and a great service to the cause of Islam and to the culture and civilization of the Medieval period which is the direct outcome of the Islamic system of education.

The major areas which have been discussed in the study can be listed as follows:

(i) The development of Education in the Islamic World from 7th to 14th century A.D.

(ii) The philosophical and ethical concepts of the Qur'an such as Reality, Knowledge, Worship of God etc. which serve as the foundation of education. Eventhough the noblest knowledge is the knowledge on Qur'an and 'Sunnah', the study of sciences dealing with worldly affairs is also recommended.

(iii) An analytical study of the schools of philosophy, which gave a guidance to the Muslim philosophers; especially the views of Plato,

Aristotle and the Neo-Platonists. However, the fundamentals of Islamic thought has its own uniqueness and it can not and should not be harmonized with Greek or any other school of philosophy.

(iv) The study of educational concepts of some environment Muslim Philosophers and educationists like Ibn Miskawaih, al-Ghazzali and Ibn Khaldun. A sociological orientation to education was given while retaining its religious character. The ideas of some more educational thinkers like al-Farabi, Ibn Sina, Ibn Suhnun, Ibn al Hajj and al-Zaruji etc. have also been discussed.

(v) A synoptic view of the aims, content, methodology and organization of Muslim education is given in the study. The important aim of education is to instill the beliefs and ideals of Islam, in the minds of the pupils.

(vi) A brief resume of the outstanding elements of the education system in the Muslim Countries in the Middle Ages has been given at last. An attempt has also been made to assess the influence of Muslim philosophers and educationists on modern educational thought and on the revival of learning in Europe.

Muslim educational thought laid great stress on the religious and spiritual aspect but at the same time it did not ignore the study of secular and rational sciences. The relevance of Muslims educational thought lies in the fact that it can imbibe in the Muslims the Islamic ideals. The stress on religious and spiritual aspects is all the more important in the world of today as religion has been completely driven away from the school because of emphasis on material progress at the expense of the moral and spiritual aspect of man. The developing countries in the third world lost both of the moral and material progress by initiating the West. So, it necessitates some changes in the system of education such as introduction of instructing the modern subjects, with modern techniques, such as natural social sciences, communication and information technology, journalism etc. so that on getting the benefit of Islamic education side by side, the student can opt for advanced studies in engineering, medicine, business and other vocations open to all other students.

Dr. Mohammad Yasin (1988) carried out a study on 'Reading in Indian History' which consisted of mainly six articles. He throws light on different aspects of Indian History through these articles. This study includes essays on 'Medieval and Modern Indian History'. The essay on 'Ibn Khaldun' formulates his conception of history, which was the earliest attempt made by any historian to discover a pattern in the changes that occur in man's political and social organization.

The historians have various approaches to the study and writing of history. Ibn Khaldun, the greatest master of all times and the Arab genius, with his tested formulae showing the way in the right direction, free from all bias, prejudices, theories and 'isms'. He has conceived and formulated a philosophy of history which is undoubtedly the greatest achievement unsurpassed by any mind in any time or place; his venture to speculate on what we should call the methods of historical research. Admirable alike by in his originality and sagacity is his profundity and his comprehensiveness, Ibn Khaldun stands above all the philosophers.

He conducted the study by dividing it into six topics; they are mainly:

i) Historiography with special reference to Ibn Khaldun.
ii) Al-Biruni as a student of a comparative religion with special reference to Hinduism and observations on India.
iii) The sub. silsilahs
iv) Indo-Islamic Architecture
v) Sayyid Ahmad Shahid of Rae Bareli
vi) Inter-sect conflict among Muslims.

The author introduces Al-Biruni as the first scientific Indologist and one of the greatest of all times, studied India and Sanskrit literature, not for the fulfillment of any worldly desires or any official inducement, but being the Hindus and their world of thought have a paramount, fascinating interest for him and he inquired with greatest predilection into every Indian subject. The author gives a clear picture of sufis. They are the friends of God. They are God-fearing and believing people. They are called as 'Hizbullah' (God's party), 'Ashab-ul-Jannat' (People of the

Paradise) and 'Ashab-ul-Maimanah' (the right-hand men) etc. in the Holy Qur'an. It is a group of people who prefer death for the sake of truth and undergo every hardship for it. The author's description on the 'Indo-Islamic architecture' is a graphic account of the evolution and culmination of the style of 'Indo-Islamic Architecture'. Never before in the history of the world, people of two creeds, radically opposed to one another in culture and civilization, ideals and tastes, came into contact as was the case in India, when Hinduism and Islam met together. It is one of the interesting facts of history, and most remarkable in the history of architecture, that they were harmonized in a happy synthesis and evolved a distinct style of their own, known as Indo-Muslim or Indo-Islamic.

The monograph on Sayyid Ahmad Shahid is based on yet unexplored sources of information. It presents a scientific portrayal of the mission and movement of Sayyid Ahmad Shahid, and highlights the evolution of two- nation theory. In this article Dr. Yasin describes the great Revolt of 1857, and states that the Sikhs sided with the British against the Muslims and the reason of it remains unanswered so far. But it was Dr. Mohammed Yasin, who came forward to trace out the reasons. The last part of the study deals with the Inter-Sect conflict among the Muslims. The article is an interesting refreshing portrayal of the different sects in Islam particularly among the Indian Muslims and gives due to the psychology and thinking of the Indian Muslims.

Mahar Abdul Haq (1991) has carried out a study on the 'Educational Philosophy of the Holy Quran'. According to him, the Holy Qur'an certainly gives the right guidance to all those who search for truth and reality; who approach it with a pure, sincere heart and a clear, thoughtful head. The bases of all knowledge, the Holy Qur'an, is perfect from all points of view, true and right guidance for the whole of humanity and for all times to come.

Man can achieve the development of his humane-ness only when 'man' has an inflicting belief in the accountability of his each and every act, whether open or secret, before an All-power authority who is transcendentally supreme to man. Human intellect will have to seek guidance and help from the higher wisdom and knowledge of Revelation which is above reason but not against it. Man holds a position of superiority among all other 'things' of 'nature'. Man is capable of self-criticism and hence self-improvement. The code of life that the Holy Qur'an presents, is the strongest and the most powerful of all man-made codes. No other law, no other legal system, no other commands and prohibitions and no other rules and regulations are as inflexible, yet progressive, as those given by the Holy Qur'an. It provides a powerful system of checks and balances through self correction and mutual friendly admonition. The Holy Qur'an, the most complete guidance for the entire humanity, is the final Revelation from the Nourisher and Sustainer of all the worlds.

The Holy Qur'an repeatedly lays stress on 'Man's own responsibility for his success or failure in achieving his higher destiny. Man was chosen by Allah to be his vicegerent on earth in spite of his imperfection. By his very nature, he is pure and good, capable of self-correction. He has the power of understanding interpreting inter – relatedness of cosmic phenomena and subduing the force of nature". The system of absolute submission of Allah's commands, to which everything in the Universe conforms so magnificently, is called ISLAM. Its values are unchangeable, its principles are unquestionable and its commands are permanent.

Mohammed Sharif Khan and Mohammed Anwar Saleem (1994) consecuted a study on 'Muslim Philosophy and Philosophers'. The authors deal with Muslim Philosophy, its origin and development in a concise, lucid and succint style. Among the Muslim Philosophers, the contemporary Muslim thinkers are also included in the study. The first session of the book is dealing with the various schools of Muslim Philosophy and the remaining part is included the contributions of Muslim thinkers. At first there comes the meaning and sources of Muslim Philosophy, Philosophical teaching of the Holy Qur'an and schools of thought in Islam. Then comes the main principles, important works and leading advocates of Mu'tazilism, Ash'arism, Tahawism, Zahirism, Ikhwan Al-Safa and Sufism. The brief introduction, Philosophy, concepts and main works of the Muslim Philosophers accounted in the book are Al-Kindi, Al-Ma'mun, Al-Razi, Al-Farbi, Abu-Ali Ibn Miskawaih, Ibn Sina, Al-Ghazzali, Ibn Bajjah, Ibn Tufayl, Ibn Rushd, Jalal al-Din Rumi, Ibn Taymiyah, Ibn Khadun, Shah Waliyallah, Muhammad Ibn Abdul Wahab, Jamal al-Din Afgani, Muhammad Abduh, Muhammad Iqbal etc.

The ideas and philosophical views of prominent Muslim philosophers are dealt with well, in the study.

Dr. Mustafa Siba'I (1995) in his collection of talks broadcast from Radio Damascus between September to December 1955 on some important aspects of Islamic civilization. Some of these talks depict the Islamic influence on education, especially in chapters 9 and 12.

He explains the establishment of schools in the Muslim world, teachers and their remuneration, the qualification of teachers who taught at various levels of education, dress of the teachers, some famous schools and their founders, and the condition of Europe at that time.

When knowledge was confined to the monasteries of the monks and hermits, and exclusion to soothsayers and priests, Islamic education was open to the public. There were societies and academies which presented learning: "this not only helped in raising the general level in improving the tastes of common people in academic pursuits but the culture is also improved".

Hussain. K. (1997) conducted a study on social and cultural life of Muslims of Malabar. Religion is characteristically seen by anthropologists as a distinctive symbolic expression of human life that interprets man himself and his society providing motive for action and also a group of associated acts for his survival. Hence religious beliefs and acts plays a prominent role in moulding the social and cultural life of the society. It operates through the thoughts and acts of individuals and since individuals are members of society, it affects the social groups and communities. For the Mappila Muslims of Malabar, religion had a prominent role in providing the community a unique social and cultured identity which differed from the indigenous society. The social system and the peculiar economic and political conditions, offered Malabar a fertile soil for the easy growth of Islam. The acquaintance with the Mappilas gave the low castes an instant to relieve themselves from the oppression and they ultimately embraced the religions of the new comers. The influx of large number of convents to the core of Mappila community resulted in continuous interaction of varied cultural elements in the formation of Mappila social structure and culture. The cultural synthesis is evident in the arts and festivals also. The Mappila arts like oppana, kolkali, parijakali and vattakkali are the Mappila versions of the folk arts of their Hindu brothers. In food, dress etc. the Mappilas followed the local pattern and local tradition. The lack of Muslim political power and the close adherence to the shari'ath gave the Mappila religious leadership a strong hold upon the community. Until the advent of Europeans the role of 'Ulama in political field was limited in acting as links between the rulers and their Muslim subjects and representing the Muslims in the various ceremonies. Mappilas of the coast had led a peaceful and admirable life, closely following their religious tenants. The atrocities of the Europeans and a lot of other reasons were compelling them to turn to militancy for which basically they were not responsible. The Mappilas closely followed the leadership on 'Ulema' and Sufis. They were generally tolerant and loyal to non-Muslims whom they have accepted as friends and to whom they were faithful and reliable in emergencies. To reform the community on modern lines and to dissuade them rebellious the authorities introduced modern education among them. All the reforms, however, brought no desired effect upon the community since the British policy of discrimination and arrogance of race and political power of the officials manifested at every step. As a whole, the Mappila character would reveal the overwhelming influence of the religion leadership as the community affected every aspect of their life and culture. This factor is evident in the community even at present to a large extent.

M. Shoyeb Ansari (1997) conducted a study on 'Education in Dini Madaris'. The study was carried out on graduate and post graduate students' curriculum, method of instruction, educational climate and evaluation in Madrasahs.

The study aims at meeting the following objectives:

1. Assessing the strength and weakness of the Curriculum, Method of Instruction, Educational climate and Evaluations in Madrasahs from students' view point.

2. Distinguishing the attitudes of students studying in Madrasahs of different philosophies and orientation.

3. Differentiating the opinions of boys and girls studying in different types of Madrasahs, ie. gender-based differences of opinions are to be highlighted.

4. To provide guidelines to educators in the field of Islamic education in bringing about reasonable modifications in curricula, method of teaching, educational climate and evaluation in Madrasahs on the basis of opinions of students of the very institutions we are talking about.

5. To narrow down the differences between modern educators and oriental *Ulama* and philosophers regarding the structure of Islamic education in tots.

There is general dissatisfaction over the centuries old, outdated curriculum, obsolete method of teaching, poor educational climate and above all unscientific way of evaluating the students in Madrasahs. But there is hardly any concrete suggestion based on scientific enquiry and research going deep into the problem to improve the situation. Moreover, those involved in teaching-learning process in Madarsahs, do not take the advice of modern educationists into account because in their estimation, these educationists are not the true inheritors of *Ilmul-Anbia* and thus have little right to speak on the matters related to the Qur'an and the Hadith. The gap between the two fractions underscores the dimensions and urgency of the problem.

Perception of students of the very institutions in which they are studying is more reliable as they are part and parcel of the system itself. If their own opinions are taken into account on items of controversy and suggestions are formulated on that basis, then the suggested modifications will be readily accepted by them. In this way, the modifications needed in curriculum, method of teaching, educational climate and evaluations in Madrsahs will bear scientific and logical basis. This also stems from the fact that educational institutions are meant for students and not for teachers or for those in the management. So whatever students themselves think about their own life and life-problem is of paramount importance and hundreds of researches reveal that maximum learning is possible if the education is student-centered and life-based, 'albeit' in Islamic perspective, for the Madrsahs.

Dr. M. Abdul Samad (1998) conducted a study on Islam in Kerala under the title 'Religious Groups And Movements Among the Muslims of

Kerala During the Twentieth Century' in the faculty of 'Islamic History, University of Kerala.

The objectives of the study were to trace out the advent of Islamic faith to the coasts of Kerala, especially at Malabar and to make a report on the cultural upliftment of the inhabitants of Malabar, the Muslims by embracing the new faith. The investigator also draws clearly a picture of all the religious and cultural movements and organizations among the Muslims of Kerala. He also explains the upliftment, reforms and awakening took place in the community by the systematic and organized approaches and activities done by the movements and organizations. The present study is to find out the historical resources that led to the origin of these groups, their ideological diversities and nature and conduct of their organizations.

It is dealt with in the thesis under twelve captions namely:

1. Islam in Kerala – Genesis and Spread.
2. Socio – Political, Religious and Educational condition of Muslims in Kerala upto the Twentieth Century.
3. Reformist Trends in Islam
4. The Islahi Movement
5. The Kerala Muslim Aikya Sangham
6. The Mujahid Movement
7. Jama'at-e-Islam Hind. Kerala chapter.

8. The Sunnis
9. The Tabligh Movement
10. Ideological Diversities
11. Ahmadiya Movement
12. Conclusion

The investigator has attempted to draw the history of Religious movements and the style of functioning of different fractions among the Muslims of Kerala. The impact of these socio religious activities as the Muslim society and the part played by these to help the transition from Medieval to Modern are discussed as conclusion. And this attempt is very much essential for a comprehensive study of the Muslim community in Kerala. Though certain authoritative works have been brought forward by eminent scholars high-lighting the socio-political life of the Muslims in Kerala, very little information is made available in respect of their religious organizations and movements. Hence the significance of the present study is worth while.

This study is carried out by Dr. A. Rhman (2000) on the basis of many advices given in Al-Qur'an and Al-hadith with the aim of bringing awareness among the Muslims, so that some steps be taken for acquiring knowledge through studies of science and technology. The title of the study is 'Islam' on Science and Technology.' Many verses of the holy Qur'an are given in this book for the purpose of establishing Islamic views on science and Technology.

The author in the study deals with Islam as a way of life, knowledge - its types and Sources, Science, Ethical values of Science, Different Branches of Science, Muhammad on general education; on useful and practical Education, Golden Age of Islamic Science, Spread of Islamic Science and Technology to the west, Indian Muslims and Science Education, Consequences of neglecting science, Down fall of Islamic science, Moral rights, Remedial measures etc.

In the beginning the author remarks that Muslims throughout the world are observed lagging behind any other community in the field of science and technology. They have not given much stress for the education of their children in these fields. Such miserable condition of the Muslims could happen only because the Muslim community as a whole has not followed properly advices and instructions of Allah and His Messenger in the field of education. There could not be any other major causes of backwardness of the Muslims in the field of science and technology if proper education policy were adopted and psychology created for science education and accordingly infrastructural facilities such as institutions were established for the education of their children.

Dr. V Sulaiman (2001) conducted a research study on 'Religion and Civilization An Analytical study of the Muqaddimah of Ibn khaldun'. He carried out an immense study on the rise and development of early Muslim politics and religion – especially on the views of Ibn Khaldun in the areas of 'Religion and Civilization'. The investigator has mainly gone through the 'life and career' of Ibn Khaldun as a whole. He described in detail the philosophical views contributed by Ibn Khaldum to the areas of Islamic philosophical thoughts. He has divided the study in seven chapters namely:

I. The Evolution, North Western Polity and society in Egypt, North Western Africa and Spain.

II. Ibn Khaldun – life and career.

III. The Muqaddimah.

IV. `Umran al Badawi (Bedoin Civilization).

V. 'Umranal Hadhari (Sedentary Civilization)

VI. 'Asabiya

VII. Religion, 'Asabiya and 'Umran

The investigator draws an elaborate picture of the celebrated masterpiece of Ibn Khaladun, 'The Muqaddimah', which fascinates the students of history on account of the scientific and philosophic treatment of the subject matter. Ibn Khaldun compares the past, the present and the future of human individual and collective life as similar to that of a drop of water with that of another.

Ibn Khaldun's Muqaddimah is the introduction to his work on history generally called Kitab al – Ibar. The Muqaddimah, originally constituted first book of history, was intended to elucidate the fundamental principles of all history which determines the true historians' re-construction of the past. 'Muqaddimah' was the original introduction and the author's first book because an independent work during the life time of the author.

The investigator concludes his study among other things saying that the involvement of Ibn Khaldun in the politics of the day was genuinely to the best of the convictions of the author and he was not a hypocrite to that effect as some Arab authorities remarked on him: He again states that there is no need of imposing our own meanings to the technical terminologies of the work such as 'Umran, Badawi, Hadhari, 'Asabiya etc. Ibn Khaldun himself has given the exact meanings of these terms in the proper places. He again states that the physical theories in 'Muqaddimah' seemed exceedingly attractive to the scientific out look of the West. But they were in no way able to rise upto the level of Ibn Khaldun who presented the study of the spiritual on a scientific or empirical level. The role that religion played in the formation of a social setup, has been clearly substantiated by Ibn Khaldun before centuries, done it by the sociologists like Durkhem. Ibn Khaldun very effectively envisaged the question of individual freedom and imperative authority of the state. Individual freedom and social harmony can be achieved by this state of affairs. In a country like India, the majority of the people devoted to religious faith, these visions of Ibn Khaladun, are of profound contemporary application.

REFERENCES

1. Irving, T.B., *Muslim Contribution to Western Culture.* Muslim World League Journal, Makkah, 1976.

2. Unus, Dr. Ilyas Ba, *Principles of Ideological Education.* State University of New York, 1977.

3. Al-Mubarak, Prof. Muhammad, *The Islamic System of Education.* M.W.L. Journal, Makkah, 1977.

4. Zuberi, Ahamed Khizar, *The concept of God among children.* M.W.L. Journal, Makkah, 1977.

5. Iqbal, Dr. Shaik Muhammed, *An Islamic Concept of Education.* M.W.L. Journal, Makkah, 1978.

6. Al-Mahdi, Sayyid Sadiq, *The Influence of Islamic thought on Europe*. M.W.L. Journal, Makkah, 1978.

7. Al-Naquib, Syed Muhammed, *Aims and Objectives of Islamic Education.* Adam Publishers, New Delhi, 1979.

8. Cader, Justice M.M. Abdul, *The Essential Features of Islamic Education*. M.W.L. Journal, Makkah, 1980.

9. Hubaiti, Prof. Abdul Khader, *The Basic Islamic Concepts of Education*. M.W.L. Journal, Makkah, 1981.

10. Rahman, Dr. A., *The Qur'anic Education Problems and Prospects.* M.W.L. Journal, Makkah, 1981.

11. Muslehuddin, Dr. Muhammed. *Philosophy of Islamic Law and the Orientalists*. Kitab Bhavan, New Delhi, 1985.

12. Khan, Mohammed Sharif. *Islamic Education.* Adam Publishers, New Delhi, 1986.

13. Alavi, Dr.S.M. Ziauddin, *Muslim Educational thoughts in the Middle ages.* Atlantic Publishers, New Delhi, 1988.

14. Yasin, Mohammed, *Reading in Indian History.* Atlantic Publishers, New Delhi, 1988.

15. Haq, Dr. Mahar Abdul, *Educational Philosophy of Holy Qur'an.* Kitab Bhavan, New Delhi, 1991.

16. Khan, Muhammed Sharif and Muhammed Anvar Saleem, *Muslim Philosophy and Philosophers.* Atlantic Publishers, New Delhi, 1994.

17. Mustafa Siba'I, *Islamic Civilization,* M.W.L. Journal, Makkah, 1995.

18. Husain, K, *Social and Cultural Life of Muslims of Malabar.* Calicut University, 1997.

19. Ansari, M. Shoyeb, *Education in Dini Madaris.* Kitab Bhavan, New Delhi, 1997.

20. Samad, Dr. M. Abdul, *Religious Groups and Movements among the Muslims of Kerala during the Twentieth Century.* University of Kerala, 1998.

21. Rahman, Dr. A., *Islam on Science and Technology.* Gauhati University, 2000.

22. Sulaiman, Dr. V., *Religion and Civilization An Analytical Study of the Muqaddimah of Ibn Khaldun.* Calicut University, 2001.

A CONCEPTUAL OVERVIEW OF PHILOSOPHY OF ISLAM AND MODERN EDUCATION

K. Abdul Waheedu "Influence of islamic philosophy on the theory and practice of education " Thesis. Department of Educaton, University of Calicut, 2003

CHAPTER III

A CONCEPTUAL OVERVIEW OF PHILOSOPHY OF ISLAM AND MODERN EDUCATION

I. PHILOSOPHY

- Educational Philosophy
- Types of Philosophy of Education
- Idealism, Realism, Naturalism, Pragmatism, Existentialism, Metaphysics, Epistemology, The Socratic Method
- Medieval Philosophy, Modern Philosophy, Indian Philosophy, Modern Indian Philosophy

II. ISLAMIC PHILOSOPHY

- Select Islamic Philosophers:
- Imam al-Ghazzali, Ibn Rushd, Ibn Khaldun

III. MODERN EDUCATION

- Theory and Practice
- John Amos Comenius
- Jean Jacques Rousseau
- John Dewey

A CONCEPTUAL OVERVIEW OF PHILOSOPHY OF ISLAM AND MODERN EDUCATION

I. PHILOSOPHY

Man has been asking several questions himself to know much more about himself and his place in the world. Speculations and thoughts from the very early times of man gave birth to philosophy, which were the answers to those questions. The views expressed by Socretes, Plato and Aristotle were the result of the questions they asked themselves.

The word 'philosophy' is derived from the composite Greek word 'philosophia' which means love or pursuit of wisdom. It is thus the endeavour to discover by systematic reflection the ultimate nature of things. Philosophy is called the science of sciences, the systematization or organization of all knowledge, drawn from empirical science, rational learning and common experience. The two main branches of philosophy are Metaphysics & Epistemology.

All knowledge was one whole in the beginning. But later, science itself got differentiated into many branches and even philosophy branched out into a number of studies. Education in the larger sense, is applied philosophy. All people think, speak, act and behave as they learn through various agencies of education. Education concerns the whole man and he becomes 'whole' or 'perfect' only when all the aspects of his life are developed equally well. In Islam philosophy rises to the level of knowledge plus wisdom.

The history of philosophy takes us back to Socretes and Plato. The reality of man's existence has been interpreted in various ways giving birth to several branches of philosophy. It emerged as a science when man found it necessary to organise his ideas and to find a meaning to the whole realm of his thought and action. Philosophy has three aspects:

i. Speculative or Conjectural
ii. Critical or analytic
iii. Prescriptive or normative

Prescriptive philosophy examines what we mean by good or bad, right or wrong beautiful or ugly etc. The analytic philosophy examines such concepts as mind, self, cause and effect etc. Metaphysics represents essentially the speculative aspect of philosophy as it studies the nature of ultimate reality. When scientific method became stronger, metaphysics was supposed to be a waste of time. Metaphysical conclusion could not be established or proven by empirical or scientific methods.

Philosophy deals with nature of man and his place in the universe, the nature of knowledge (or epistemology) and axiology (or the science of values). The theory of knowledge or epistemology examines how the knowledge originated (i.e. source of knowledge), the use of knowledge, and what is involved in the process of knowledge.

Knowledge according to philosophy can have five sources:

i. Knowledge Originated from God (revealed knowledge)

ii. Authoritarian knowledge – (received from authorities)

iii. Intutive knowledge – (derived by means of intuition)

iv. Rational knowledge – (derived by reasoning)

v. Empirical knowledge – (derived by experimentation)

In the realm of knowledge all these types are being used. When we consider the question of religious knowledge, the scriptures are the sources of revealed knowledge which is unquestionable and untestable.

Most of our factual knowledge is authoritative as it comes from authoritative sources which are as such acceptable. This knowledge is rather encyclopaedic.

Intuitive knowledge is the knowledge which a person gets as a result of intuition or a sort of sudden flash of insight. This knowledge cannot be atributed to any special source as it occurs on a subliminal level. Intuition is supposed to be the most intelligent of all kinds of intelligences.

Rational knowledge springs from reason which can be subjected to intellectual organization, but it has its limitations in the sense that rational process can be influenced by subjectivity.

Empirical knowledge is derived through the senses that it is the knowledge gathered through five sense organs and composed of ideas found in accordance with observed facts. Modern scientific knowledge is empirical.

General study of values is known as axiology. Three questions araise in the study of values: whether they are objective or subjective, constant or changing and hierarchical in nature or not.

Educational Philosophy

Application of philosophy to education can be called educational philosophy. Education, being a life-long process, can be any act or experience that has a formative effect on the mind and character of the individual. Education in the sociological sense is an instrument for transferring and conserving the cultural values of the society and education can be a process and a product - as a process it is an act of educating whereas as a product it is the knowledge, ideas, techniques etc. we receive as a result of the process. Educational philosophy is a part of general philosophy because most of the major problems of education are at the bottom philosophical. Therefore educational philosophy can be speculative, prescriptive or analytical in nature or it can be originated from any source mentioned above.

Types of Philosophy of Education

The important philosophical views which have influenced modern education are Idealism, Realism, Naturalism, Pragmatism and Existentialism etc.

i) Idealism

Idealism is concerned with 'idea' more closely than with 'ideal'. It is a doctrine or a set of doctrines, to the effect that reality is in some way mental. Idealism is contrasted primarily with Realism, though also with materialism. According to Idealistic view, the universe is spiritual in the sense; it depends on God. There are different ways of looking at reality, none of which is more correct than the others. It is not primarily concerned with ethics or conduct, though certain ethical views have sometimes been associated with it. It takes many forms, but its central point is that there is only one ultimately real thing, the Absolute, which is spiritual in nature.

Sometimes a distinction is made between *subjective* and *objective idealism.* 'Subjective Idealism' is of the view that the only reality is ideas in the mind, especially the human mind. Berkely used *immaterialism* instead of 'Subjective Idealism'. '*Objective Idealism,*' like absolute idealism, applies mainly to forms of idealism which place reality outside the human mind. Shelling, Hegel, Kant etc. are some of the Idealists.

ii) Realism

The doctrine of Realism means that universals have a reality of their own, an extra-mental existence. The more definite, fixed and external the status of the universals, the more absolute is the Realism. 'Realism' gets its sense largely from what it is contrasted with. Any view can be called realist which emphasizes the existence, or role, of some kind of thing or object (eg. material objects, propositions, universals), in contrast to a view which dispenses with the things in question in favour of words (nominalism), ideas (idealism, conceptualism), or logical constructions (phenomenalism). The aesthetic realism emphasizes the nature of things as they are in themselves, not as we see them. A realist art forms aims to portray things as they are not as mediated by some attitude, etc. of the artist. The chief apostles of this doctrine after Plato and Aristotle are Plotinus, St. Augstine, Boethius, Avicenna, Hegal, Russel, Moore etc.

iii) Naturalism

It is a general philosophical view centring on the belief that the universe is all one, in the sense that all objects in it, and all aspects of it, are equally accessible to study by scientific method. Naturalism nowadays mainly denotes a related ethical doctrine, to the general effect that there is no unbridgeable gulf between ethics and other studies. It takes two main forms, that ethical terms can be analysed into non-ethical terms, and that ethical conclusions can logically be derived from non-ethical premises.

Naturalism holds that all explanations must finally make reference to objects and events in space-time. There is no non-natural order to which appeal can be made. The position differs from materialism in denying that all phenomena can be reduced to matter in motion. The qualitative aspects of experience – eg. the distinctions proper to logic, ethics and aesthetics – are regarded as valid and in some important sense irreducible. The promoters of this idea are Santyana, Woodbridge, John Dewey, Morris Cohen, Ernest Nagel Horace Kallen and Hook etc.

iv) Pragmatism

Pragmatism is a philosophical movement of the late 19th and 20th centuries whose emphasis lay in interpreting ideas through their consequences. It originally developed as a theory of meaning by Peirce who was concerned with the meaning of concepts affecting the intellect, especially scientific concepts, rather than those confined to the senses or emotions. This theory can be thought of a looser form of operationalism.

Pragmatism is thought of as a theory of truth. Truth is what would be believed; it is the limit where belief is finally stabilized. W. James developed the theory and he differed from Peirce by including, and emphasizing the effect of concept on our senses and emotions. He seems to mean that the truth is whatever we ultimately find believeable or consistent. But our emotions influence what we do ultimately find believeable or consistent. The philosophers labelled pragmatists include John Dewey, Schiller, William James, Lewis, Le Roy and Ernest Nagel etc.

v) Existentialism

It is a philosophical movement concentrating attention on the human situation. It is a movement primarily associated with Kierkegaard, Sartre, Nietzsche, Marcel, etc. Its exponents have widely differing outlooks, in religion and politics as well as in philosophy, but share certain general themes. Existentialists regard the being which applies to men as something which men only attain sometimes. Existentialism describes the human conditions on two philosophical footholds, in metaphysics and ethics. It views that men are active and creative while things are not. Men must choose the principles on which they choose. They are not like things, already determined. 'Existence precede essence' for men. The reality and nature of freedom are major concerns for existentialists. In elaborating what being is for men, and how men are related to the world, recent existentialists have been strongly influenced.

Existentialist writing both reacts against the view that the universe is a closed, coherent, intelligible system, and finds the resulting contingency a cause for lamination. In the face of an indifferent universe we are thrown back upon our own freedom. Acting authentically becomes acting in the light of the open space of possibilities that the world allows. Different writers developed very different ethical and metaphysical system as a consequence. Existentialism turns into scholastic ontology; into a dramatic exploration of moments of choice and stress; it becomes a device for reinventing the relationships between people and God.

The main proponents of this doctrine are Kierkegaard, Nietzsche, Unamuno, Jaspers, Marcel etc.

Metaphysics

Metaphysics deals with ultimate reality. According to materialism nothing but space-filling physical objects are ultimately real, while idealism holds that only spiritual beings are ultimately real and that other things are to be explained as ideas.

Plato and Aristotle represent two different attitudes towards the world. To Plato, this world is the world of change and is unreal, while Aristotle holds it to be real and the change only a succession of forms. Plato was an idealist, Aristotle was a pragmatist.

Socrates was convinced that one could act only on the basis of the truth. Plato tried to construct a theory of knowledge. What knowledge was available, how we could obtain it, and why it was true. Platos' viao was that knowledge consists in apprehension of those aspects of the world which never change, never alter. The world contained such constituent elements, which he called 'ideas' or 'forms'. The way to obtain complete and true knowledge, is, first, to give up any reliance upon sense information and turns instead to examining the intelligent world through the aid of one's reasoning power only.

Epistemology or Theory of Knowledge

The philosophers have tried to develop a theory of knowledge to account for the source, basis and certainty of the knowledge. Some philosophers of rationalistic view have tried to find a completely certain procedures of human reasoning. They sought for knowledge in the strongest possible sense under no circumstances, it could be false. Usually the rationalists found that such knowledge could not be discovered in sense experience, but only in some mental reason.

Kant took the position that sensations are the only source of our knowledge of objects in the empirical world. He viewed sense experience as conditioned by the constitution of human mind which contained certain forms of cognition or understanding by which the fleeting impressions of the senses are absorbed, co-ordinated and integrated. For him, reason is yet superior to experience as the source of knowledge. Experience gives us nothing but separate sensations and events which may alter its sequence in the future. It is mind, an active agent, which moulds and co-ordinates sensation into ideas and transforms the chaotic multiplicity of experience into the ordered unity of thought. Sensation is merely an awareness of a stimulus. Sensation does not arrange themselves into an order. There is the co-ordinating power that receives them and moulds them into sense and that is mind. Thus sensation is un-organised stimulus, perception is organized sensation, conception is organized perception. 'Perception' without conception are blind. Kant argues that pure or theoretical reasons are applicable only to phenomena that appear to such experience, objects of faith a free and immortal soul, a benevolent creator can never be proved by reason. 'Faith must be put beyond the reach of reason'.

Bertrand Russel said, "No one has succeeded in developing a theory of knowledge which is both credible and consistent".

The conclusion is that neither sense nor reason can be the basis of sure knowledge. Then the origin of sure knowledge can be revelation which above is the source of real knowledge and can guide us to the ultimate reality. The attempts of senses and reason, in solving the ultimate problem, end in failure because the finite cannot grasp the ultimate. God above possess the final knowledge of things. He is the creator and sustainer of the universe.

The Socretic Method

Socretes was not interested in natural sciences. Being a man of consuming interest in ideas, he naturally turned to philosophy. Though he was acquainted by the leading wizards of Sophists like Pythagoras, Gorgias, Hippias etc., he encountered them. He accepted skepticism, logic etc. from them. He derived his logical tactic from theSophists and this is known as Socretic method, because of his masterful, inclination with it. He seriously questioned other men's opinions till exposing their shortcomings, inappropriateness or absurdity.

He used to x-ray and elucidate ideas by exposing false and malformed opinion and by reforging them on the anvil of reason. This was his dialectic method, simply the art of making careful distinctions in the science of precise definition.

Socretes never bothered on the opinions of his adversaries. According to them he had a clever tongue to discredit their keep sake beliefs. He left them no replacement. He took recourse in the logicians slight of hand. He would cunningly alter the meaning of the terms in midstream leaving no room to suspect by anybody. When asked he was never willing to answer his own questions, instead he flatly refused. His critiques remarked that he knew nothing because of his statements like, "you shall not hear another word from we till you yourself state what justice is". He views him as a God-appointed midwife, assisting to deliver knowledge into the world, but forbidden to be its maker. He views man as the measure of all things". He was convinced that knowledge is the indispensable basis of truth on which all men, regardless of their personal disparities and diversities, could agree. As a teacher he did not venture to give instruction in almost everything. His mission was to promote morality, and it was to this and that he directed his skill of turning ideas inside out. At all times he refused payment for his instruction on the ground that he had taught nothing. Socretes delivered his thoughts for the making of a good society. He persuaded his people to make themselves upright and decent to think straight. He stressed on preparing his disciples for the concrete realities they would have to face in everyday living. For guidance, he recommended to make them literate and to keep them fit both as civilians and as soldiers. He invited students' attention to arithmetic, geometry and astronomy alongwith his plea for instruction in the dance, the trial art and poetry. He pleaded for ethics for a happy and satisfactory relationship with others. The historical position of Socretes is determined by his dialectics of definition and his original conception of science as universally valid knowledge. These views became the basis of the philosophy of Plato and Aristotle' (P.39).

Medieval Philosophy

It designates the philosophical speculation that occurred in Western Europe during the Middle ages: from the fall of the Roman Empire in 4th and 5th century. Christian thinkers such as Ambrose, Victorinus and Augustine began to assimilate Neoptatomism into Christian doctrine in order to give a rational interpretation of Christian faith. Thus medieval philosophy was born at the decline of Greek and Roman philosophies and it was enriched with Christianity and Islamic Philosophy.

Modern Philosophy

Western philosophy in the Middle Ages was primarily a Christian Philosophy, clarifying the divine revelation, devoting itself to the institutional tastes of the Roman Catholic Church. The major philosophical achievements of the 13th and 14th centuries were the works of church men, the professors at the universities of Oxford & Paris.

Three novel mechanical inventions from the East were introduced to the West during the Renaissance of the late 15th and 16th centuries.

These were gun powder, block printing from movable types and the compass. The renewed study of classical literature became the foundation of the philosophy of Renaissance. Humanism emphasized the centrality of man in the universe, his supreme value and importance. The science and philosophy of the Renaissance built its foundations on the three formulations; the principle of Empiricism, the advocacy of mechanistic science and the faith in mathematical explanation. The 18th century was clearly the 'century of philosophy par excellence'.

Indian Philosophy

It was mainly based on Hindu religion. It mainly includes orthodox and unorthodox systems. The significant ideals discussed in them were the nature of the world (cosmology), the nature of reality (metaphysics), logic, the nature of knowledge, (epistemology), ethics and religion. Whether knowledge arises from experience or reason was main theme discussed among them.

Vedic hymns, Hindu scriptures, the Upanishads (Hindu Philosophic treatises) etc. contain Indian speculations about nature, life, mind, and the human body etc. Indian philosophies contain a diversity of views, theories and systems. Indian philosophers give immense importance to intuitive knowledge. They are concerned with the concepts of self or soul (atman), works (karma) and salvation (moksha) and their interrelations. Sankara was a leading Advaita Vedauta Philosopher.

According to him, reasoning should be allowed freedom only as long as it does not conflict with the scriptures. The interpretations like the adhidaivata (pertaining to the deities), the aitihasika (pertaining to the tradition), the adhiyaygna (pertaining to the sacrifies) and the adhyathmika (pertaining to the spirit) etc. prevailed in the Upanishads.

The ancient Indian tradition classified the classical systems (darsanas) into orthodox (astika) and unorthodox (nastika). Astika accepts the authority of Vedas and nastika does not. The Sankhya system did not involve belief in the existence of God and Yoga (a mental psychological physical meditation system) made room for God not on theoretical grounds but only on practical considerations. The PurvaMimamsa of Jainini, the greatest philosopher of the Mimamsa school ignores the questions of the existence of God.

Modern Indian Philosophy

The 19th century in India was a period of great social and religious reform movements. The newly founded universities introduced Indian intellectuals to Western thought. The Western oriented ideas served to generate a secular and rational point of view and stimulated social and religious movements like 'Brahma Samaj movement' founded by Rammohan Roy. The great saint Ramakrishna Paramahamsa of Calcutta taught an essential diversity of religious paths leading to the same goal and his famed disciple Swami Vevekanandan gave an intellectual form to his teachings.

The first Indian graduate school in philosophy was founded in the University of Calcutta during the first decades of 20th century. The German philosopher Kant and Hegel were the most studied philosophers in the Indian Universities. The great Indian Philosophical thinkers are Sri Aurobindo, Mahatma Gandhi, Rabindranath Tagore, Sir Muhammed Iqbal, K.C. Bhattacharrya and Sarvepalli Radhakrishnan etc. Rabindranadh Tagore placed love higher than knowledge, Mahatma Gandhi emphasized Ahimsa as his ideal and Dr. Muhammed Iqbal wrote "The truth however is the mater in sprit". Dr. S. Radhakrishnan was an interpreter of Indian thought to the Western world. The most original among the modern Indian thinkers, is K.C. Bhatacharya. He rejects the conception of Philosophy as a construction of world view and in his view absolute freedom from objectivity is a spiritual demand.

II. ISLAMIC PHILOSOPHY AND EDUCATION

Islamic Philosophy aims at the balanced growth of the total personality of Man through the training of Man's spirit, intellect, rational self, feelings and bodily senses. The training imparted to a Muslim must be such that faith is infused into the whole of his personality and creates in him an emotional attachment to Islam and enables him to follow the Qur'an and the 'Sunnah' and be governed by the Islamic system of values willingly and joyfully so that he may be raised to the status as 'Khalifatullah'. This type of education will promote in man the creative impulse to rule himself and the universe as a true servant of Allah not by opposing and coming into conflict with nature but by understanding its laws and harnessing its forces for the growth of a personality that is in harmony with it.

Knowledge of contemporary issues, especially in the field of scientific and social development and information must be given to pupils at all levels. The educational system is to be shaped so as to facilitate social mobility. Thereby all barriers will be removed to give equal opportunity to all Muslims to attain the highest stages in society according to their capacities.

All education is self education, that is to say, it is a change within the soul, or an education not only by 'the self' but also of 'the self and 'for the self'. The creation of the Universe and of Man cannot be without a purpose. Man's duty, here is to advance this purpose, undergo toil and struggle for it and thereby achieve his own high destiny progressively but assuredly. Education concerns the whole man and the whole man becomes whole only when all the aspects of his life-material, moral social, spiritual, in fact all-are developed equally well.

The processes through which education takes place are instruction, training and indoctrination. The Qur'anic methods of education are: 'Zikr' and 'Fikr' (Remembrance and contemplation), 'Saum' and 'Salat' (Fasting and canonical prayers) as training and 'Amrun bil Ma'ruf' and 'Nahyun 'anil munkar' (mutual admonition and counselling for recognized behaviour and prohibition from unapproved conduct) as indoctrination.

According to Islamic philosophy, human nature is basically good though it has the tendency to fall down to the lower state of animality also. It is the right philosophy of education alone that can bring intelligent order and discipline, true sense of responsibility and efficiency into the chaotic world situation. The whole of the Universe is manifestation of the Beauty, Goodness, and Truth inherent in Allah and this manifestation continues forever without a beginning and without an end. The aim of educational philosophy is (no more and no less, than) to search for, establish and identify this Beauty, world of matter and motion and to provide all the means for the expansion of each individual fraction to the extent to which its potential has the capacity to evolve.

Some verses from Holy Quran, certain traditions (Hadith) of Prophet Muhammad and some sayings of famous sages of Islam, denoting the importance of knowledge are given. A clear picture on how Islamic ideology treated knowledge and learned men can be traced from these quotations.

Quranic verses on Learning (Knowledge)

- "Say, Are those equal, those who know and those who do not know" (39:9).
- "Read in the name of thy Lord who created, Created man from a clot, Read: it is thy Lord, the most Bountiful who taught by the pen. Taught man that which he knew not" (16:25).

- "It is only those who have knowledge among His slaves fear Allah" (35:28).
- "Only men of knowledge draw right conclusions" (80:28).

Prophet on Knowledge

- 'Acquire knowledge because he who acquires it in the way of the Lord, performs an act of piety; who speak of it, praises the Lord, who seeks it, adores God; who dispenses instruction in it, bestows alms; and who imparts it to its objects, performs an act of devotion to God'.
- 'Acquire knowledge and learn to do so with tranquility and dignity and be humble in the presence of those who are teaching you'.
- 'Acquire as much knowledge as you wish: for by Allah, you will not be rewarded for gathering knowledge until you practise (what you have learned)'.
- 'Seek wisdom and it wouldn't harm you in any way from which vessel it came out'.
- 'Seeking knowledge is an obligation of every Muslim. A learned man whose knowledge is beneficial is better than a thousand worshippers'.
- 'Knowledge is the life of Islam with pillar of faith and whoever gains knowledge, Allah gives him His fullest reward'.

- 'Learning is a treasure house whose keys are queries. Show modesty to those from who you acquire knowledge and those whom you give knowledge'.
- 'The ink of the scholar (will be weighed against) is more holy than the blood of the martyr on the Day of Resurrection'.
- 'One who leaves home in search of knowledge walks in the path of God; the angels offer their wings to the seekers of knowledge'.
- 'To one who travels in search of knowledge, God shows him the way to Paradise'.
- 'To listen to the instructions of science and learning for one hour is more meritorious that attending the funerals of a thousand martyrs, more meritorious than standing up in prayer of a thousand nights'.

Saying of the Sages on Knowledge

- Words of Hazrat Ali: Knowledge is better than wealth. Knowledge guards you, but you are guarding wealth. Knowledge dispenses justice while wealth seeks justice. Wealth decreases with expense while knowledge increases with expense. A learned man is better than one who prays and fights in the way of God. Hazrat Ali said in poems.
- Nothing is more honourable than knowledge. While the kings rule over the people, the learned rule over the kings.

- Hasan Basari said: The ink of the learned will be weighed against the blood of the martyrs and then it will be found that the ink of the learned is heavier than the blood of the martyrs. That thing which remains with you even if your boat capsizes, that is knowledge.
- The death of one thousand persons who pray all the nights and fast all the days is a lesser calamity than the death of one learned man who is versed in lawful and unlawful things of God.
- Ibn Mubarak said: A man is learned till he searches for knowledge. When he thinks that he has knowledge, he becomes ignorant.

The chief exponents of Islamic thinking mainly discussed here are Imam Ghazzali, Ibn Rushd and Ibn Khaldun. An attempt is made to examine their contributions to different faculties of thought and spheres of life. From the influence of their unparalleled thought during Middle ages, the Western Europe made an intellectual upliftment mainly in the philosophy and the areas of education.

Select Islamic Philosophers

Imam Ghazzali (1058-1111 AD.)

Imam Ghazzali was born in 450 AH (1058 A.D.) in the village of Taberan, in the district Taus in Persia and his name was Abu Hamid Muhammad, His title is 'Hujjathul Islam' or 'proof of Islam' and 'Ghazzali' is dynastic title. 'Ghazzali' is said to be the name of a village in the district of Taus in the province of 'Khorasan' in Persia. According to Maulana Shibli Nu'mani, his ancestors had the business of weaving (Ghazzal) and therefore he retained his family title 'Ghazali' (weaver).

Abu Hamid Muhammed ibn Muhammad ibn Ahmed al-Ghazzali is one of the greatest and most original thinkers in the history of Muslim Philosophy as well as in the history of human thought. He travelled for nearly 10 to 11 years and spent his time in reading, writing and teaching. He wrote nearly 400 books. The most celebrated one among them is 'Ihya Uloomiddin' (Revival of Religious Learning). Tahafatul Falasifa, Akhlakul Abrar, Maqsadul Falasipha etc. also are important.

'Ihya Ulumuddin' (Revival of religious sciences) is the master piece of Imam Ghazzali. Remarks on the book by his contemporaries are: 'Ihya is near the Quran': A book like Ihya was never compiled before'. If all the lights of knowledge of the world are extinguished, they can be revived from Ihya. The great saint Shaikh Abdullah Idres committed to memory the whole book. Shaik Ali read it 25 times from first to last and at the end of each reading gave a feast to the students and poor. Many disciples of the Imam learned 'Ihya' by heart. Many saints regarded the book as a result of 'Ilham' or inspiration. Mr. Watt says: Ghazzali has sometimes been acclaimed in both East and West as the greatest Muslim thinker after Muhammad and he is by no means unworthy of that great dignity.

Ghazzali's book 'Ihya...' is divided into four sections: 1) The book of Worship, 2) The book of worldly usages, 3) the book of destructive evils 4) and the book of constructive virtues. Ihya has five special characteristics when compared to other books; They are in the words of Ghazzali: Firstly I have opened by the grace of God what they closed up and I have written in detail what they kept secret. Secondly I have arranged what they kept scattered and thirdly I have brought together what they made long and corrected what they approved. Fourthly I have deleted what they repeated and repeated what they deleted. Fifthly, I have made this book easy to understand after disclosing the subtle matters' (1).

On completion of his education, he turned his mind to gain spiritual heights and the circumstances leading to it were recorded. He interacted with the peoples of all sects, thoughts and ideas. Among the men, with whom he used to conduct discussion, arguments and debates were the Deists, the Materialists, the Naturalists, the philosophers, the Shias, the Sunnis, Zindigs, Magians, Scholastic theologians, Christians, Jews, atheists, fire-worshippers and idol worshippers etc. He spent two years in solitude at Damascus with divine services, meditation and 'zikr. Then he made three promises: 1) He would abstain himself from attending the Darbar of any ruler, 2) He would never accept their presentation or rewards, 3) He would not join any religious debates. He fulfilled these promises till his death. He died at his native village Taberan in 505 AH (IIII AD).

From the very beginning Al-Ghazzali had an intense desire for truth. The thirst for knowledge was innate in him. From his boyhood he broke the fetters of tradition and authority and freed himself from hereditary beliefs. He was attracted by the diversity in beliefs and the variety of doctrines. Each sect believed itself to be in possession of truth and salvation. By this experience, he felt the need of searching the truth and in this connection he ascertained the foundations of certitude and the complete knowledge of things and it left no room for doubt or error. While Descartes held that reason was competent to explain the ultimate reality, al-Ghazali like Kant disbelived in the absolute powers of reason also and found it incompetent to answer the metaphysical questions.

Al-Ghazzali strongly challenged the then prevailing philosophical views based on cause and effect theory. The relation between cause and effect is a relation of necessity as where there is the cause, there is the effect and vice-versa. The relation between cause and effect is the relation of one to one the same cause, the same effect and vice versa. He proclaimed that there was no compelling necessity in the relation between cause and effect. Any two events in nature considered as cause and effect are merely possible existents and there could be no necessary connection between them. The analysis of al-Ghazzali on cause and effect is one of the most original contributions to the history of human thought. He considered thought as an organ for the knowledge of reality. According to philosophers the past becomes linked with the present and the present with the future through a necessary connection so that the relation between cause and effect is such as it is impossible to have an effect without its cause.

Two important aspects of theory of emanation:

(i) The relation between cause and effect is relation of necessity: where there is the cause there is the effect and vice versa.

(ii) The relation between cause and effect is the relation of one to one. The same cause, the same effect and vice-versa.

Al-Ghazzali strongly challenged these statements. According to him there is no necessity to be seen here between the one and the other. Naturally, there could be no necessary connection between cause and effect. Hence the causal relation is a natural, possible relation and not a logically necessary relation. An effect is always observed as happening alongwith the cause either conjoined with it or immediately succeeding it, but never has it been observed to be happening through the cause. Al-Ghazzali opines that all philosophical assumptions, speculations and hypotheses should be judged and verified with reference to facts, for, otherwise, they would be empty and meaningless. Reason can not demonstrate the existence of God, nor the immortality of the soul. Therefore, the questions with which we are deeply concerned end in doubt.

Al-Ghazzali said: "I arrived at truth, not by systematic reasoning, and accumulation of proofs, but by a flash of light which God sent into my soul"(2).

He refutes the ability of philosophy on the basis of its own assumptions to reach truth and certainty, and reduces it to an ancilla of theology. Al-Ghazzali is a man for all seasons; for the Sufis, Al-Ghazzali is a Sufi; for the theologians he is a theologian; for the legalists, he is a jurist. He said "to refute, one must understand". He had studied all the schools of thought. He had established a credible synthesis of philosophy, theology, law and mysticism in his own person. By working back to first principles, al-Ghazzali could put the disciplines themselves in order.

It is a peculiarity of Imam al-Ghazzali that his life and work are so intimately connected that they could not be separated. According to him, one can not find the truth except in matters which carry their evidence in themselves. Al-Ghazali could defend the arguments against the existence, the unity, the simplicity and the incorporeity of God. He established the God's being as the Creator and the Sustainer of the universe. He proved the spirituality and immortality of the human soul. By his philosophical doctrines, he claimed for the God's knowledge of the particulars, the eternity of the world and the denial of bodily resurrection. He had the habit of free thinking: he wrote: "It has always been my practice, as a youth and as a man, to thirst for knowledge of the true nature of things .... So that I can be freed from the bond of imitation"[3]. Al-Ghazzali believed that personal knowledge should spur one to good deeds which please God and lead to salvation. In order to put end to the self-indulgence, he turned to Sufism for answer to his question about certainty. He sees that doubt means more than 'confusion of thought' or suspension of judgment. According to al-Ghazzali, 'Reasons is like the power of sound vision which sees well, and the Qur'an is like the sum irradiating light everywhere. Hence reason with revelation is light with light'. Whoever lacks a penetrating inner vision has only the superficialities of religion'. However, reason is the ideal way of restoring confidence in the facts and aims of revelation. Kant, like al-Ghazzali thought that through speculation or theoretical reason it is impossible for the philosophers to prove the existence of God and of soul and its immortality. Al-Ghazali marked a note of voluntarism, in oppsotion to the Aristotelian, and understood the ultimate, reality in terms of 'will' rather than 'thought'.

Al-Ghazzali believed that human nature is not immutable, but can be moulded by moral instruction. He formed ideas on the ideal way to bring up and educate the young. Natural inclinations and instincts should not be suppressed entirely because they are needed for essential tasks in life. Desire was created for some benefit and is an essential part of nature. A child's soul has been created imperfect but capable of being made perfect through moral instruction and nourishment with knowledge.

According to Al-Ghazzali the human will is not absolutely free since it is subject to the deliberation of the mind. Man's ability to act is also subject to ability. The three elements of will, ability and action seem to have been predestined from eternity as part of an inescapable determinism. Man's will is based on his ability to distinguish between good and evil, and this distinction is one kind of rational understanding. The action which the will carries out seems to be subject to the judgement of reason. In every man there is a particular will and reason which guide him in his practice. Actions in this world seem to be the result of the divine volition which creates in the heart of man a will, deliberation and motives. Every event in this world is in the final analysis, a completion of the violation of God.

Al-Ghazzali opined that the mission for which man was created is that of knowledge and worship and for this he needs a safe society to live. A country's secutiry is the basis for Government and essential for the collective welfare of its citizens. Government must be established on the principles of unity and sovereignty. He emphasized the states' rights of control and sovereignty. The ruler's duty is to care for his people and to commit himself to the ideals of fairness and justice the ruler should ensure that the law of the land is applied equally strictly to all citizens.

Al-Ghazzali's views on Education

Al-Ghazzali has put forward his philosophy of education on the bases of his personal experiences. The philosophical views of Ghazzali and Plato are alike. According to al-Ghazzali, it is the prime duty of every Muslim to search reality through the knowledge in accordance with Holy Quran. He divides knowledge into two parts: dogmatic and non-dogmatic. The dogmatic knowledge is that which come to us through prophets. All the other sections of knowledge relate to non-dogmatic. Al-Ghazzali divides again the knowledge related to hereafter into two categories: the knowledge related to Affairs. The revelation is the extreme and supreme of all other knowledges. Any person who has not benefited all from this source of knowledge is at a great loss. The revelation is the name of light. When the heart is clear from evils, the light appears. Knowledge related to affairs tells the condition of heart. It is knowledge of conditions.

According to al-Ghazzali, the objective of education is utility. He used wide meaning of utility which prevails over the material and spiritual aspects. His utility theory consists of individual as well as social phenomena. According to him, the objective of education is formation, construction and completion of manners so that man can distinguish between good and bad and abstain from evil. On the one hand it will formulate the character of individual and on the other hand it will reform the society. He considers three aspects of human spirit; knowledge, anger and lust. The objective of ethics is to create moderate and proper harmony in these three aspects so that by their mixture a good human being and a better character may come into existence.

He suggested that subjects should be taught in their order of utility and importance. He recommended life-oriented and activity - oriented education. It was in agreement with the views of John Dewey, an eminent expert in education and founder of 'pragmatism'.

Imam Ghazzali recommended that previous knowledge of pupils may be taken into consideration while giving learning activities in the class. The Western Educational thinkers emphasized and advocated the necessity of previous knowledge of pupils. Imam Ghazzali recognized the method of teaching easy things first and difficult things later on. The Western thinkers presented it later on the way of easy to difficult. He has also suggested the use of teaching aids to make the lesson more interesting and effective.

The teachers should treat the children with parental affection. The prophet says: 'The teacher should be so considerate and affectionate as a father to his son'. The teachers are responsible for their morals and custodians of their character. They should estimate the abilities of students. The modern educational experts also accept these principles of education for the success in life.

He recommended certain manners to be observed by the students:

1. The Pupil should keep himself free from impure habits and evil matters.

2. He should reduce his worldly affairs and keep aloof from kin and kith as acquisition of knowledge is not possible in these environments.

3. He has not to take pride or exalt himself over the teacher but rather entrust to him the conduct of all his affairs and submit to his advices as a patient submits to his physician.

4. He should adopt first what the teacher says and should not argue about the different mazhabs or sects.

5. He should not miss any branch of knowledge. He should try to become perfect in them.

6. He should not take up all branches of knowledge at a time, but should take up the most important one at first as life is not sufficient for all branches of knowledge.

7. He should not take up new branch of learning till he has learnt fully the previous branch of learning, because it is requisite for the acquisition of further knowledge.

8. A student is to know the causes for which noble sciences are known – nobility of its fruit and the authenticity of its principles.

9. He has to purify mind and the action with virtues, to gain proximity to God and His angels and to live in the company of those who live near Him.

10. He should pay attention to the primary object of knowledge. He may not try to enjoy the bliss of this world and that of the next world alike together.

He advocated primary education for women and it will help them to provide proper training and education to children. He did not consider higher education essential for women and he recommended Home Science education for women. Aristotle and Roussean were of the same view, in this issue.

He emphasized the physical education of the children. He advocated for proper physical growth and development of the children. So, we can say that Imam Ghazzali was in agreement with the saying, 'sound mind in a sound body'.

It can be said that Imam Ghazzali had approached the educational philosophy and problems of his own days with his point of view and his suggestions were very much similar to those presented by the Western educational thinkers and philosophers like Commenius, Russeau and John Dewey.

Imam Ghazzali was always a man of independent thinking. As the world is advancing with evernew ideas, and scientific discoveries and thereby the Imam revived truly the religious sciences and gave them as impetus never given by his predecessors in such manner. He saved Islam from the attack of alian ideas and devilish thoughts that impreceptibly entered into Islam and clearly showed their fallacies and misconceptions. For this reason he was given the title of 'Hujjathul Islam' or the proof of Islam. His thoughts influenced the thinkers who succeeded him. The Almighty God blessed him with the necklace of reason and intellect. So the true belief and ideology of Islam were protected from the strong current of irreligious and misguided thoughts.

The method of teaching generally followed in his time was reading from the text or lecture by the teacher. There was little scope for pupil's participation in the teaching-learning process. Role-learning was stressed. Reform of the method of teaching was attempted by al-Ghazzali. The organization of education, planning of teaching work, status of teachers, duties and responsibilities of teachers and students, the examination system, granting of degrees and distribution of certificates etc. were discussed by him.

Ghazzali said: What I mean by this knowledge is the knowledge for attaining the ultimate object of life. What I understand by the science of outward behaviour and usage is the knowledge of practical religion attended with actions in accordance with that knowledge. The science of revelation is the ultimate object of those who search after truth and the most coveted matter in the eye of the extremely truthful, and the best way of acquiring knowledge of worldly usages. The Holy Prophet did not speak anything about the science of revelation except through signs and symbols, because he knew that wisdom of men to understand it is very little. The science of the practical religion are of two kinds: open science of the actions of the physical senses and the secret science of the functions of the heart. The actions which keep connections with the physical sense are the actions of habits or usages of life. The heart which comes from the unseen world and is removed ultimately from senses is influenced by either the praiseworthy virtues or the blameworthy vices. In short, the science of practical religion is divided into open and secret sciences. The open science belongs to the senses; the secret science belongs to the condition of heart and its qualities.

As the minds of the people are attracted to the science of medicine for preservation of the health of body, so also it is necessary that the minds of the people are attracted to the treatment of the diseases of soul and mind in expectation of a happy and prosperous life in the next world which will be ever-lasting. Physical happiness is short and transient as compared to spiritual happiness in the hereafter. Physique is mortal while soul is immortal.

Acquisition of Knowledge

Many Quranic verses and Traditions of Prophet Muhammed (S.A.), stress the importance of knowledge and learned people. Imam Ghazzali placed the rank of the learned men and their honour much high. According to a report of Ibn Abbas, the rank of the learned is seven hundred times more than that of the believers and the difference between the two ranks is the distance of the path of five hundred years. It is learned that the learned are the heirs of the prophets and there is no rank above the rank of prophethood and there is no honour higher than its inheritance. By the report 'wisdom increases the honour of the noble and exalts a servant as high as to raise him to the level of kinds', it is understood that even in this world the fruits of learning can be enjoyed. Imam Ghazzali views that the prophet has linked knowledge with prophethood and he belittled the rank of the learned man without action eventhough is worshipping always and he would not have worshipped has he not possessed knowledge. The rank of the learned is next to that of the prophets and higher than that of the martyrs.

Those who exchange the religion for the world are the meanest. Knowledge distinguishes men from animals and it is only for knowledge that men are honoured. This honour is not due to man for his physical strength because a camel is physically stronger than a man. This honour is not for his large body as the body of an elephent is bigger than that of a man. This honour is not on account of his bravery as a ferocious beast is braver than a man. This honour is not for his strength of too much eating as the stomach of an ox is bigger than that of a man. This honour is not for his strength of sexual urge as the sexual urge of certain other creatures is greater than that of man. This honour of man is on account of knowledge and intellect. When the heart is not given wisdom and knowledge for three consecutive days, it dies. The food of the heart is knowledge and wisdom. As food keeps the body alive, these two things keep the heart alive. He, who misses knowledge has got his heart diseased and its end is its death but he does not understand it. Nobody is born learned; learning is to be acquired. "To discuss about learning in a portion of night is dearer to me than to keep up awake throughout the night in prayer"[(4)].

According to Qur'an, teaching is binding on Muslims; concealing truth is unlawful. Who is better worship by mind, the fountain head of acquisition of knowledge, can not be attained without the removal of bad habits and evil attributes. Death of the heart is the punishment of a learned man. The death of the heart is due to search of the world with the actions of the hereafter.

Ghazzali considers this world and the next world as diametrically opposed to each other. All the learned men who translate their learning into practice are in error except those who are sincere. Those learned men who are sincere are in fear till they come to know their ultimate good end.

He views that 'a grievous crime indeed against religion has been committed by the man who imagines that Islam is defended by the denial of the mathematical sciences'. Similarly religious people who reject the philosopher's science of logic give the impression that religion rests on the rejection of logic. The natural science or physics of the philosophers does not need to be rejected.

Al-Ghazzali was one of the greatest thinkers and geniuses the world has known. The focus of his thoughts and the principal aim of his teachings and of his learned discourses attracted people to morality. He well realized that the society of his time was steeped in the glitter and worship of this world and hence realized the necessity of tremendous moral teaching and religious injunctions. His unique scholarship, wide experience, sharp insight, deep thinking and wonderful sense of judgement went a long way to give a direction to the disillusioned society. His thoughts and great writings were instrumental in giving a clear direction to the disillusioned Muslims of the Middle Ages, particularly the intelligentsia of that period who were greatly influenced by Greek philosophy.

Ibn Rushd (Averroes) (1126)

Abu-al-Walid Muhammad ibn Ahmad ibn Muhammad ibn Rushd was born at Cordova in Spain in 1126. He was described as one the profoundest commentators of Artistotle's works. He belonged to a renowned Spanish family which produced scholars of jurisprudence and law. He was a learned scholar, and from the very beginning of his career, never forsook free thinking and contemplation. He wrote about 78 books, mostly philosophical. His important work in philosophy is 'Tahafatu' t-Tahafut, rejecting the arguments of Al-Ghazzali's philosophical views in 'Tahafut', dealing with the self-destruction of the philosophers.

Ibn Rushd acquired all knowledge available in that period. He had knowledge of Medicine, astronomy and jurisprudence etc. Eventhough he possessed no novelty and not founded any new school of thought, the style of his criticism distinguished him from his contemporaries. Although Ibn Rushd was a scholar of philosophy and medicine he excelled in philosophy. He was also a scholar of jurisprudence and astronomy. He studied all the sciences and literature of his age and was also cognizant of the science and literature of the ancient times. He always kept himself engaged in search of reality. He disagreed with Ibn Sina and Al-Ghazzali, on the basis of the appreciation and rejection. His distinct style shows his genius, scholarship and excellence. His style also reflects his distinguished personality. He wrote three types of commentaries on Aristotle, short (in poetry), medium and long.

In Europe he is famous for the theory of the 'Unity of the Intellect'. It is really an expression of the Neoplatonic concept that true knowledge consists in the identity of the known with the known. He was also associated with 'two truths' theory; this contends that his doctrine was that there is one truth for philosophers, which is philosophy, and another for the masses, which is religion. Ibn Rushd actually sought to harmonize the Quran and revelation with philosophy and logic.

He was a great thinker and (consensus) educationist. His habit of study was such that he used to read sixteen hours a day even when he was seventy. It is said that he left no book of any prominent author unread. He surprised all his contemporaries at 40 by his musical proficiency in philosophy and fiqh.

His reputation, fame and wealth increased under the patronage of Caliph at Mansur. Al-Mansur was forced to banish him from the country by the pressure couped against him from the common people misguided by the orthodox 'Ulama', who became antagonistic towards him on his unparalleled fame and approval.

Ibn Rushd is famous in the Medieval West as 'Averroes' scholar of the Quranic Sciences, and the natural sciences (physics, medicine, biology, astronomy) theologies and philosophy. Ibn Rushd approached philosophy through the theoretical sciences. He gives the reasons for divergences, demonstrates their motivations and justifies them. His original contribution is to stress the importance of adherence to truth. Men understand it through the ways which gain their assent; the majority consent to something because of what they themselves are, rather than because of what the thing itself is. Their truth is subjective, which they can accept and adopt, so that their subjective attitude does not lead them into erroneous representations. According to him, the majority of the people should be taught only the general methods which the Qur'an has revealed and used for them. But the special method which the Holy Book suggests for those who are capable of it and for scholars. It is the fact that different types of mind can arrive at the same truth; it is the practical agreement of two methods in order to arrive at a single practical conclusion, one of them being no more than this, the other based also on a theoretical demonstration and a speculative knowledge.

Ibn Rushd considers time, whether it is created or eternal. This recalls very early discussions which go back to Plato, Aristotle etc. He examines critically the argument that the infinite cannot be crossed, which demands a point of first departure if one is to arrive at the present event. This is true for sequences in a straight line, but not for cyclic sequences where an initial point of departure is not apparent. He states that it is essential to prove first that the void exists and that it is infinite and eternal, otherwise another void would be necessary to contain it.

Ibn Rushd distinguishes clearly between the Qur'anic doctrine and the theories of the theologians who raise problems on which the Qur'an is silent. Thus on knowledge: God knows what He has created, for there exists in creation an order and a wisdom which shows that the Creator has knowledge. He points out the contradictions on the one hand human action obviously depends, both for its cause and its execution, on external and internal conditions created by God; but on the other hand, we are the authors of our own acts since "it is evident that God had created in us faculties by means of which we can acquire things which are opposed by nature" which proves that freedom of choice exists.

The Five Divine Presences: a metaphysical doctrine of the degrees of reality in descending order: Hahuit the Godhead the absolute reality, tatut-the reality of Being, Jabarut-the world of Angels, Malakut-the subtle world, and Nasut the human world. As a universal metaphysical doctrine it reflects the nature of things, and is no more the creation of human thought than the rings of Saturn are the creation of Galileo.

Both the science and revealed scripture are sources of truth. A reconciliation must be found for "truth does not oppose truth, but accords with it and bears witness to it". This stance provides a straight forward denial of the theory of double truth' wrongly attributed to Ibn Rushd by some European Averroists.

Some of his great works are:

1. Mabadi'ul – Falasifa (Introduction to Philosophy).
2. Destruction of Destruction, Philosophy.
3. On the Agreement of Religion and philosophy.
4. Kulliyat-fil-Tib – a work on medicine
5. Kas;liful – Adellah, scholastic
6. Bidayat at-Muthahid wa-Nihayat-al-Muqtasid

Besides writing some 38 philosophical works, he was also a distinguished physician. His writings included 16 excellent medical works, captioned as 'Kulliyat fi-al-tibb, a medical encyclopaedia of seven volumes dealing with anatomy, diagnosis, materia medica, pathology, physiology and general therapeutics.

He is known as a commentator among European scholastics. Ibn Rushd agrees with Aristotle's belief in the eternity of the world. He says, 'Pure matter and forms are created' Matter contains in itself the capacity of taking form. Both matter and form are eternal and necessary and permanent. It does not resolve, but an apparent motion is connected with the stars fixed in it. Ibn Rushd differs from Ibn Sina, who believed in the universe, but also as the matter of the forms. He opines that the sun and the stars affect the earth by their light. The supreme being loves Himself and has knowledge of His own existence. In His essence, He knows all things and perceives them in Himself. His knowledge embraces the whole universe.

No Muslim thinker influenced the West more than Ibn Rushd.

His main ideas opened the door to the European Renaissance:

1. Allegorical interpretation of the scriptures.
2. The theory of two truths
3. Pan-psychism which implied immortality of the Universal soul of humanity, and morality of the individual soul,
4. Eternity and potentiality of matter and
5. Emancipation of women

Ibn Rushd's theory of two truths, combined with the doctrine that matter is eternal and potent to produce all from within itself. For his theories, De Wulf calls Ibn Rushd the Doctor of Anti-scholastics.

Averroism became rapidly the ruling mode of thought in the West. From the end of the 16th century Averroism remained the prominent school of thought. His writings became prescribed studies in the University of Paris and other institutions of higher learning.

Ibn Rushd was a rationalist and an exponent of Aristolelian Philosophy: Each heavenly body possesses its intelligence or soul which is its form. Human intelligence is immaterial, immortal, abstract and separate from the individual. It is an emanation of the universal soul, and is temporarily individualized. Soul is an energy which gives life to matter. He held that recompense after death would be spiritual and not physical. He believed in the perpetuity of creation, and the process of its continuous renewal. He held that God knows with His own essence the entire world in its generality and its multiplicity. He regarded the soul as an abstract entity exempt from all materiality. He considered that the soul was ultra sensitive fluid. He criticized the theories of Al-Ghazzali. His writings stirred up the critical reaction throughout the Islamic world.

Averroes taught the intelligence, emanation and the regular gradation of the spheres. All forms are a series of emanations, which have their principle in God. God is the prime mover, Who formed the universe by extracting the forms from matter, which is co-eternal with Him and independent of Him in existence the active intellect is the principle of human cognition. It is the last and least perfect of the emanations, an immaterial and eternal principle, distinct and separate from man. The passive intellect which attributes to the human soul, is an organic faculty, which ceases in death. Averroism was the most formidable intellectual foe of Christianity in medieval times. It found many adherents in the universities. The doctrine of the double truth and of the monistic intellect survived until the seventeenth century.

Ibn Rushd was not concerned with conflicts between philosophy and theology. But he attacked the views of fallible theologians and half-educated philosophers who merely confused people. His concern was to find harmony between philosophy and scripture itself. He outlined a system of doctrines for reasonable Muslims and refuted many erroneous teachings of the theologians.

In his book 'Tahafut' he says: In the sequences of causes it is necessary that the present effect is the result of all these causes. If they are all infinite, it can not exist. But it is not necessary, for all the past revolutions of the sphere to be added together in order for the present revolution to take place. Thus it can be said that 'the circular – movements of the past and the future are non-existent'. It is not possible really to separate essence and existence; the distinction is made only in thought.

Averroes admits the existence of the true possible which leads to the necessary possible, which he implies to a necessary reality based on a true possibility, that is on a potentiality. The same is the agent which translates the potentiality into the actuality. There is no other action than this. God makes actual the potentialities which are in the world. The world in its totality is not a pure possible which receives existence. It is an organized whole necessary through the interplay of the causes which are its laws, and the proof of this is that everything in it is subjected to movement.

To understand his thought and method, we have to go through his explanation of the Aristotelian doctrine. Among the possible interpretations he chooses that which suits his own ideas.

Averroes gives great importance to the accidental in all the phenomena of this world. He realizes, as Aristotle, that although the world as a whole is necessary, it includes within itself some realities whose existence merely occurs with a greater frequency. This pre-supposes the existence of realities which occur with a lesser frequency. There must therefore exist in this world accidental chances. No doubt, the relation of the cause to the effect is always necessary; but a cause can interfere in a natural process which, as such, is a stranger to its causality. 'As for a cause which results in an effect of change, this is not at all the cause of a natural movement. The natural causes are ordered towards a natural end.

Ibn Rushd takes up a view that the material intellect exists and the separate agent intellect is another form in the material intellect. The material intellect is in itself generable and corruptible. It seems that Averroes considered the habitual intellect to be the way in which the gent intellect is present in us, that is in that part of our soul, which is the material intellect. Its action in us has a beginning and an end; like acquired knowledge in the scholar, it is not continually in use.

He did not reject the revelation nor did he minimize the nature of prophethood or miracles. His political beliefs were that man must be free from all oppression and injustice.

He expounds the doctrine of eternity as two kinds: eternity with cause and eternity without cause. The world is eternal because of a creative and moving agent eternally working upon it: God, on the other hand, is eternal without a cause. The priority of God to the world does not consist with reference to time: God's existence does not imply time, since He exists solely in timeless eternity. God's priority to the world consists solely in His being its cause and that from all eternity. The soul must be distinguished from intellect. Intellect is the faculty through which the man knows the eternal truths, without the media of sense organs, like fundamental laws of thought, ultimate values, etc. These come to it from the over mind of the universe, ie, the active intellect, which is their real source and origin. He does not agree with the immortality of the individual intellect. After perishing the body at death, the intellect, being imperishable, goes back to be merged once again into active intellect to live there in eternity alongwith other intellects. Thus the immortality of the intellect is not individual but collective, it is not personal immortality but corporate immortality.

Soul is a driving force and sustains life and effects the growth of organic bodies. It is a kind of energy which gives life to matter. It is not altogether free from matter like intellect, but on the contrary, is closely associated with it. His belief in personal immortality is fully confirmed by his views regarding the nature of bodily resurrection. Ibn Rushd explains that it is the scholar's rational faculties that constitute his means of doctrinal reasoning. Therefore, the mind is the ultimate tool of knowledge, prepared as it is by God to deduce his presence and to reason in earthly matters as well. This divine qualification renders the human mind continuous in space and time, and open across all nations to a common knowledge. Therefore we must make use of what those who preceded us had, whether they share our religious beliefs or not. He insists to use rationality to pursue knowledge of all kinds. Any suppression of the mind would be a clear violation of this order.

Being an advocate of intellectual liberty and openness to other nation's cultures, he posed to threat to the rigid minds of scholars. One of the foremost figures of Arab civilization, be became known as the 'Prince of Science' the master of jurisprudence, mathematics, medicine and above all philosophy. In the Middle Ages, his ideas influenced the transformation of thought in medieval Europe. The last of the great

Muslim thinkers, his beliefs were to have an effect on the minds of many Middle Ages' intellectuals, living well beyond the boarders of Moorish Spain. Ibn Rushd has been encouraged to discuss Greek philosophy freely and wrote his commentaries on the works of Aristotle. He regarded Aristotle as embodying the highest development of human intellect. He understood, interpreted and analytically discussed Aristotle's true thoughts more than any of his Muslim predecessors or contemporaries. He argued that the milk sister of religion, philosophy confirms and does not contradict the revelation. He placed intellect above everything-else. In doing so he surpassed Aristotle in over-emphasizing the intellect. He tried to correlate the intellect with revelation.

To Averroes, the world has been moving from eternity and has an Eternal Mover (Muharrik), which is God. Matter and form are inseparable except in the mind, there is a hierarchy of existing beings and forms. Matter is always in motion, where as the intellect is motionless and perceives itself. The soul is one in all men, but is maintained separately by bodies, and its relation to the body is like the relation between form and matter. In his essay 'The Harmony of Religion and Philosophy' he asserts that 'since philosophy is true and the revealed scriptures are true there can be no disharmony between religion and philosophy'. He believed that to the simple masses, one must speak of religion, but to the enlightened few, one may disclose scientific truth.

Ibn Rushd's ideas were to ignite the fire of change in Christian Europe. It was through the translations of Ibn Rushd's 'Commentaries' on Aristotle into Latin and German, the revival of true Aristotelianism took place in the West. Roger Bacon acknowledged that Scotus was largely responsible for the most important change in the history of medieval thought, which resulted from the introduction of Ibn Rushd's Aristotle to the Christian West. The subject of harmony between reason and faith was passed on to Christian Europe, giving impetus to the development of rationalism. Ibn Rushd was able to recover the genuine Aristotle which the West, by way of translation, was later to discover. Through his commentaries on the works of Aristotle, Ibn Rushd, known in the West as Averroes, played a leading role in the revival and development of Christian scholasticism. In spite of the fact that many Muslim scholars found his approach too rationalistic, his writings were a mine of ideas and information for Christian philosophers, creating turmoil in the minds of many medieval European intellectuals. For four centuries from the 12th to the 16th, his works were subject to heated dialogue among the scholars in Christian Europe, forcing the Church to modify its teachings. Many of the free-thinking Latin Christian thinkers of Europe felt him to be one of their own, even though misplacing his name to 'Ave Ruiz'. However, his views had a very profound affect on medieval Christian theology.

Unlike in Europe, where there was on the one hand providential history and on the other hand social and Secular history, Ibn Khaldun combined both. Averroes tried to do the same. Ibn Khaldun and Averroes came out of the same cultural formation. Both, when their ideas reached Europe, the providential or Islamic dimensions were stripped away. So, they became social historians and secular materialists.

Ibn Rushd has been held as one of the greatest thinkers and scientists of the 12th century. According to Philip K. Hitty, Ibn Rushd influenced Western thought from the 12th to the 16th centuries. His books were included in the syllabi of Paris and other universities till the advent of modern experimental sciences. His books on philosophy had a far reaching effect on European philosophers. For several countries until the Renaissance his theories and conclusions on several philosophical issues were the main guidelines. Many scholars regarded him as the father of Western philosophy. The influential university of Padna became the centre of Averroism. In Oxford, he was established as the interpreter of Aristotle. Francis Bacon honoured him as a midpoint between Aristotle and Ibn Sina.

Yet the Averroist conception of the eternity of matter and God's communication with things through the medium of an active intellect continued to be a vital factor in European belief until the dawn of modern experimental science. For hundreds of years, Averroes and Averroism provoked intense arguments in the academic circles of Christian Europe.

Ibn Rushd made the greatest impact on European philosophy. In the history of Europe he is known as Averroes.

Ibn Khaldun (1332-1406) (732-808 A.H.)

Abdur-Rahman Abu Zayd Ibn Muhammad Ibn Muhammad Ibn Khaldun was born in 1332 in Tunis and died in 1406 AD. He was a most profound scholar, original thinker, the greatest intellectual of the century who propounded a most remarkable programme for sociology and theory of history. He exercised a far-reaching influence on the science of history, philosophy, literature and education. He is reckoned with those intellectual giants like Socrates, Plato, John Locke, Rousseau, Herbert, Spencer and John Dewey. Ibn Khaldun is renowned for his Muqaddimah (Prolegomena), a mine of information on sociology, geography, state and democracy, political economy, culture and education.

Ibn Khaldun is generally regarded as a historian, philosopher, sociologist, economist, politician and pedagogue. Above all he is treated as the father of the science of history. His fame was as sociologist and a theoretician of history. Innumerable studies have taken place on his life and works and it caused the most varied and even the most contradictory interpretations. He was one of the first to make a really critical study of the nature, limitations and validity of human knowledge.

He took a very modern and utilitarian view of life and education. He believed in the transfer of training and thought that every sort of mental training exercises a wholesome influence on the development of mind. Learning through discussions and seminars was the most suitable method for acquiring knowledge. He emphasized the method of discussion between the teacher and taught.

Ibn Khaldun was the first historian to assess the elements of progress in social and educational environments. He propounded the theory of gradation which reflects the most modern view of education. He recommended keen observation and deep thinking. He suggested the importance of thinking for the purpose of learning. He recommended 40 minutes periods for school children because the teacher cannot hold the attention of the students for more than a limited period.

Ibn Khaldun had made a most modern suggestion that the purpose of early education should be mainly to develop the power of expression, by laying proper emphasis on the study of language. He recommended that the teacher should proceed from known to unknown, from simple to complex, from easy to difficult. He thought the socialization through education can also be achieved by educational excursion and tours for acquiring direct and extensive knowledge experienced in life, society and environment. According to him language learning is nothing but a matter of habit formation.

Ibn Khaldun's main work of universal value is the 'Muqaddimah' it is an introduction to the historian's craft. Thus it is presented as encyclopaedic synthesis of the methodological and cultural knowledge necessary to enable the historian to produce a truly scientific work.

Ibn Khaldun is generally regarded as a historian, sociologist and philosopher. His view on history influenced Toyenbee and probably through him modern education. He is often called as the 'Father of Historiography' and the 'Father of Modern Sociology'. Eventhough he wrote history, he did not write historical narrative. His subject matter was the philosophy of history and the sociology of knowledge. He was an acute observer of human nature. He noted the tendency to admire and respect power, so that conquered people often adopt the habits and customs of the conquerors, even to the extent of adopting their dress. In studying human nature, he was led to analyze the significance of sleep and to consider the prophetic character of certain dreams according to traditional psychology. His great work the Muqaddimah or prolegomena is the introduction to his Kitab-al-' Ibar (Book of Examples) and the collection of Origins of the History of the Arabs and Berbers'.

According to Ibn Khaldun there existed a recurrent pattern in the history of nomads and sedentaries, who represent a primordial division of human existence in the world; he holds that there is a natural state of tension under the best conditions. Moreover, town-dwellers inevitably tend to fall into decadence and moral curruption, from which the nomads are preserved by the ardous nature of their daily lives.

At the beginning the world was an endless space, and time was eternity, only a rhythm, a return to the same movement. With the fall, change enters into the society, eventually change begins to dominate it, and time becomes a duration. The Biblical story recapitulates the history of the world as the absorption of space by time as duration.

Ibn Khaldun observed in the 'Prolegomena,' the dynamics of the two poles in human history, still in their traditional phase, a waving taking place between nomads and sedentaries.

"We can compare Ibn Khaldun with al-Ghazzali; both had a highly critical attitude towards philosophy, and both strongly maintained that is not through reason alone but through religious experience that we apprehend the nature of ultimate reality"[(5)].

The Philosophical views of Ibn Khaldun are available in an introductory volume on methods of history, called 'Muqaddimah i.e. 'Prolegomena' before his work of voluminous of history of the world. A student of philosophy and a student of history, both can benefit from this alike.

Ibn Khaldun was an astonishingly clear thinker. It is true that his behaviour was dictated by ambition, the desire of power, a taste for adventure. His adventures could be seen as only the unfruitful and calculated search to save Islam.

Muqaddimah

Ibn Khaldun's main work, of universal value, is the 'Muqaddimah'. As the title indicates, it is an introduction to the historians' craft. It is presented as an encyclopaedic synthesis of the methodological and cultural knowledge, necessary to enable the historian to produce a truly scientific work.

In his preface to the 'Muqaddimah', Ibn-Khaldun begins by defining history – which he expands to include the study of the whole of the human part, including its social, economic and cultural aspects- defining its interest and setting out the rules of good and sound criticism. This criticism is based essentially on the criterion of conformity with reality, that is of the probability of the facts reported and their conformity to the nature of things. Hence the necessity of bringing to light the laws which determine the direction of this current. The science capable of throwing light on this phenomenon is a science which may be described as independent which is defined by its object: 'human civilization and social facts as a whole'. The main part of the 'Muqaddimah' is the detailed exposition of the new and independent science which the author had perceived. This exposition is divided into six long chapters and mathematically arranged. Chapter 1: a general treatise on human society. It is an outline study of the influence of environment on human nature, an ethnological and an anthropological study. Chapter 2: On the societies of rural, and generally speaking, fairly primitive, civilization. Chapter 3: on the different forms of Government, on states and institutions. Chapter 4: on the societies of urban civilization, that is of the most developed and sophisticated forms of civilization, Chapter 5: on industries and economic affairs in general. Chapter 6: On scholarship, literature and culture matters in general. He remarks that one has the impression of being present at a new creation, at an actual renaissance and at a new world. Thus the need is felt for someone to make a record of the situation of humanity and of the world. He accepted observation as his main tool in this work of analysis. He was much concerned about the problem of knowledge and it led him finally to a refutation of philosophy. In short, Ibn Khaldun rejects the traditional speculation of the philosophers, only to replace it by another type of speculation, the steps of which are more certain and the results more fruitful since it is directly related to concrete facts.

It can be found in the Muqaddimah the early beginnings of a number of disciplines which have become independent sciences only very recently. Ibn Khaldun was the first who introduced history as a science. 'The differences which are seen between the generations in their behaviour are only the expression of the differences which separate them in their economic way of life'. This statement can be compared with an equally famous one of Marx: 'The method of production in the material matters of life determines in general the social, political and intellectual process of life'.

According to Ibn Khaldun, the aim of history is to describe the story of human civilization. It is essentially the record of human society, its growth and decay under different geographical, economic, political, religious or other cultural conditions. A historian is expected to have developed an insight into the laws governing the structure of human society and its transformations. He should have a scientific approach towards the understanding of historical changes. He should not be biased by no speculative or theological prepossessions. He is required to base his explanations strictly on some empirical evidence, i.e. his own observations and experiences and those of others. While searching for the causes of historical changes he should carefully look into the climatic, territorial, occupational, economic, social, religious and other cultural conditions of the people under study. He has a keen realization of sociological laws governing the course of history.

Ibn Khaldun was undoubtedly a sociologically minded historian. A grasp of laws on social phenomena would enable the sociologist to understand and predict the direction of social processes around him. Societies are essentially dynamic like the living organisms. The social forms change and evolve. Ibn Khaldun holds to be the contact between different peoples or groups and the consequent mutual initiation and assimilation of cultural traditions and institutions. Ibn Khaldun conceived of the growth, development and decline of nations, societies and cultures similar to those of human organism in that a period of progress is necessarily followed by a period of regress and extinction. He realized the regular rise, growth and fall of societies and cultures according to the inevitable laws of casuality.

Ibn Khaldun views that :

- Philosophy is competent enough to understand and interpret the truths of religion and is thus capable of being reconciled with it.
- The salvation of human soul is possible merely through abstract philosophical thoughts.
- In the graded series of emanations from God to the world is directly related to the first intelligence.

According to Ibn Khaldun, the existing opinion that 'true happiness and salvation of human soul with abstract philosophical contemplation' is contrary to actual experience. But he opines that philosophy is a perpetual quest leading nowhere; the more you study it, the greater the confusion and doubt that it brings. Instead of bringing happiness and salvation it might bring misery and curse.

Like Kant, Ibn Khaldun believes metaphysics to be an impossibility. The knowledge of the phenomenal world in the last analysis is based on the perceptual experiences. But the knowledge of a percepient is limited by the number and capacity of his sense organs. We should learn to feel humble regarding our own knowledge of the phenomenal world, for after all the number and the range of our own perceptual experiences are also much limited. There may be beings in the Universe better equipped for the knowledge of things, both in range and quality than we are.

Ibn Khaldun describes "reasoning as a faculty through which we form concepts out of a number of percepts and consequently move from the less general concepts to the more general ones. It is through the processes of analysis and synthesis that we form a general concept from the particular percepts. The more general a concept is, the simpler it is, for, as the denotation of a term increases, its connotation decreases. Here, human reason comes to its limits; it cannot go beyond these ultimate concepts, nor can it explain their mystery"(6).

Ibn Khaldun remarks that reasoning is a faculty through which we find the casual connection between things and trace a chain of causes and effects. The more intelligent a person is, the greater the number of things or events that he connects through casual *nexus*. The universe is an architectonic whole and the things are bound together the chain of causes and effects. As we run through this entire gamut of casual connections we come ultimately to the notion of the first cause, for the series of causes cannot go in regressing infinitely. But one fails to understand the nature of the first cause; the reason comes to its limits once again. However, the philosophers knew that they could not know everything through reason.

The Muqaddimah (Prolegomena or introduction) can be regarded as the earliest attempt made by any historian to discover a pattern in the changes that occur in man's political and social organization. Rational in its approach, analytical in its method, encyclopaedic in detail, it represents an almost complete departure from traditional historiography, discarding conventional concepts and diches and seeking, beyond the mere chronicle of events, an explanation – and hence a philosophy of history.

In rejecting idle superstition and denouncing uncritical acceptance of historical data, Ibn Khaldun adopted a scientific method totally new to his age, and used a new terminology to drive home his ideas. That he was fully aware of the originality of his thinking and the uniqueness of his contribution, illustrated by the many references he makes to his 'new science'.

The Muqaddimah begins with man's physical environment and its influence upon him. This is followed by an analysis of primitive social organization, the character of early leadership, and the relationship of primitive human societies with each other, as well as their relationship to the higher, urban form of society. Then government of the state, the highest form of human social organization, is discussed in general and that of the caliphate, the special Muslims case, in particular. This includes an exposition of how changes come about in the dynasties ruling a given state. It is argued that the urban life is the most developed form of human association and civilization. All aspects of higher civilization are examined in detail: commerce, the crafts, the arts and the sciences, considered both as pre-requisites and consequences of urban life.

The centre of Ibn Khaldun's world is man. Man is dependent on his physical environment. The best conditions for human existence obtain in the middle regions of the earth, between its northern and southern extremes. Environmental differences affect and shape man's character, his appearance and his customs.

Ibn Khaldun stresses that the individual human being can not secure all the things necessary for his livelihood without co-operation from someone else. To make all things he needs, a man by himself would require longer than the time he can keep alive without them. The ability to think, God's special gift to man, enables human beings to co-operate each other. In this way each individual accomplishes something from which his fellow men can prompt. Full co-operation results in a complicated social process called 'urbanization'. Hence the dictum 'Man is political by nature' – he needs this kind of social organization in order to satisfy his material and other requirements. But, basically man is an animal, proper order among men co-operating in such social – organization can exist only when they are governed by justice in the form of a restraining influence that keeps them from devouring each other. A person with such restraining influence upon others is called wazi by Ibn Khaldun.

As soon as some kind of social organization is formed, civilization results. When a social organization grows more popular, a better civilization also develops. This growth in numbers with a corresponding growth in civilization finally culminates in the highest form of sedentary culture man is able to achieve.

There must be some factor, some incitement, for the desire for co-operation to exist on a larger scale among some human beings than among others. These are the causes of differences in the size, quality and influence of different human social organizations. The group to which an individual feels most closely attached is his clan or tribe, the people with whom he shares a common descent. No group can retain its superiority, nor any leader his dominant position in the group, when their former solidarity (group feeling) is no longer there to sustain them. The leader who enjoys the support of a sufficiently effective 'asabiyat' (solidarity) may succeed in founding a dynasty and gaining royal authority for himself and his family.

Man is able to develop the crafts, the arts, and the sciences. This bias towards luxury, however, carries with it the seeds of the dynasty's eventual decay and disintegration. The desire of the ruling group to gain exclusive control over all the sources of power and wealth brings about a conflict between the dynasty and public men. According to Ibn Khaldun all dynastic history moves in cycles. As it draws nearer to decay and disintegration, the dynasty shrinks inwards under the pressure of the challenging outsides and his group until it finally collapses. All the higher civilizations are preserved by maintaining 'aptitude' or habit. Through continuous practice, one individual may master a craft or a science, thus making it his habit; and since the acquisition of habits is a matter of education and training, habits can be passed on to others willing and fit to learn them.

The introduction deals with the great merit of historiography, offers and appreciation of its various methods and cites historians' errors.

The First Book, Kitab al-'Ibar' deals with civilization and its essential characteristics, namely, royal authority, government, gainful occupations, ways of making a living, crafts, and sciences, as well as the causes and reasons thereof.

The Second Book deals with the history, races, and dynasties of the Arabs, from the beginning of creation down to this time. This will include reference of such famous nations and dynasties contemporary with them, as the Nabateans, the Syrians, the Persians, the Israelites, the Copts, the Greeks, the Byzantians, and the Turks.

The Third Book deals with the history of the Berbers and of the Zanatah who are part of them; with their origins and races; and in particular, with the royal houses and dynasties of the Maghrib.

'The Muqaddimah' is the Introduction and Book One of the World History, entitled 'Kitab al-'Ibar' of Ibn Khaldun. In the Muqaddimah, the various aspects of civilization, that affect from human beings in their social organization, are explained as royal authority, gainful occupation, sciences and crafts, all in the light of various arguments that will show the true nature of the varied knowledge of the elite and the common people, repel misgivings, and remove doubts.

Man is distinguished from the other living beings by certain qualities peculiar to him:

1) The sciences and crafts, the ability from which distinguishes man from the other animals and exalts him has thinking being over all creatures.

2) The need for restraining influence and strong authority, since man can not exist without them.

3) Man's efforts to make a living and his concern with the various ways of obtaining and acquiring the means of life. This is the result of man's need for food to keep alive and subsist.

4) Civilization means that human beings have to dwell in common and settle together in cities and hamlets for the comforts of companionship and for the satisfaction of human needs, there are things that affect civilization essentially in as far as it is social organization.

The Book one of 'Kitab al –' Ibar' reveals his views on philosophy. It contains six chapters. The first chapter deals with centres of Human civilizations, oceans, rivers and zones etc. The human civilizations centred in the southern quarter of earth. Its temperate and intemperate zones are described. The influence of air and climate upon the colour and character of human beings, the availability of food materials in the inhabited regions and its effect on the human body and character etc. are discussed.

The other chapters from two to six include the notes on Arab population the life conditions of the tribes, the natural groups and forms sedentary peoples and their civilizations, the reason to the just and unjust conditions of men and so on. Ibn Khaldun deals with administration of the states and mentions that a sign of royal authority is a person's eager desire to acquire praiseworthy qualities and vice versa. The dynasty and its greatness, the extent of its territory, the royal authority, the caliphate and government ranks, the length of its duration, the authority etc. are narrated alongwith the statement that human civilization requires political leadership for its organization. Also described on countries and cities and that towns and cities are the secondary products of royal authority. The ways of making a living and gainful occupation with its aspects, the crafts, the sciences, the study and acquisition of it are illustrated in detail. He had his own views on education, and critically analysed the education of his time.

Ibn Khaldun's writings reveal that he was interested not only in philosophy as such but in practical aspects of philosophy as applied to history of the human race, society, administration, business, religion etc.

Philosophy is a field of study which is worthwhile and necessary for the history of philosophy in order to prove that (Islamic) philosophy is an integrated part and a link in the chain of philosophical tradition. Ibn Khaldun took a materialistic position in his studies; and his predecessors were to be found where materialism was evident, where the quest had been for a natural, rational explanation of the universe. Ibn Khaldun's science of human culture is something essentially new, that Ibn Khaldun was the first to attempt to formulate social laws. He interprets history as an eternal cycle. Apart from the connections with the philosophical tradition and with the situation of Ibn Khaldun which will become apparent herein, whether such a view is compatible with the basic religious attitude toward history and whether Ibn Khaldun's view of history is at all Islamic, Ibn Khaldun's central term 'asabiyah', which be regards as the driving force in the development of society and to determine the relation of then force to other social factors. Since history means the origin and operation of human culture, Ibn Khaldun's theory is fundamentally different from ancient or medieval theories of history.

The great significance of Ibn Khaldun has been almost universally acknowledged. Philip K. Hitti speaks of Ibn Khaldun as the discoverer of the true scope and nature of history, as the founder of sociology, and as one of the greatest historians of all times. Flint exclaims: "Neither the classical nor the medieval Christian world can show one (name) of nearly the same brightness... as a theorist on history he had no equal in any age or country until Vice appeared... Plato, Aristotle, and Augustine were not his peers and all others were unworthy of even being mentioned alongwith him".

'I completed the composition and draft of this first part (Muqaddimah) before revision and correction in a period of five months...'[(7)]. Ibn Khaldun remarks on historiography: 'How can you develop criteria to distinguish between a true, and a false report, when you get conflicting reports'? He looked into the problem of causality. There has to be a certain cause and effect; a relationship of logic. History is not haphazard. This fitted completely with his Islamic world outlook. History is now the realm of our freedom. Man can save or damn himself. There is always the Qur'an for guidance. He distinguished between the Divine on the one hand, and the natural and human on the other. The divine we accept, the natural and human comes under the domain of reason, and man has to apply his reason. Hirodotus tried to find some kind of pattern to history. Ibn Khaldun made the first concerted effort to find certain patterns in human history. This becomes sociology and philosophy. Many Western educational thinkers like Toyenbee are influenced by his views in the field of Philosophy and historiography. However he is regarded as the 'Father of Historiography' and 'Father of Sociology'.

The remarks made by the great thinkers of the world, on Ibn Khaldun as follows:

"….. In the Maqaddimah to his Universal History he has conceived and formulated a philosophy of history which is undoubtedly the greatest work of its kind that has ever yet been created by any time or place. In his chosen field of intellectual activity he appears to have been inspired by no predecessor' – Arnold Toynbee. 'As regards the science or philosophy of history, Arabian literature was adorned by one most brilliant name. He was admirable alike by his originality and sagacity, his profundity and his comprehensiveness' – Robert Flint (British historian) "Ibn Khaldun was a historian, politician, sociologist, economist, a deep student of human affairs, anxious to analyse the past of mankind in order to understand its present and future…one of the first philosophers of history. A forerunner of Machiavelli, Bodin, Vico, Comte and Cournot"[8].

It is an established fact that Ibn Khaldun is the father of the philosophy of history and the founder of sociology. Ibn Khaldun is remarkably modern and scientific in his thinking.

III. MODERN EDUCATION
Theory and Practice

The word 'modern' includes the Western knowledge of sciences and system of education in modern times. Education in Europe during the 'Middle Ages' was totally influenced by the Christian Church and religious Scholars. There was scarcely any influence of an individual philosopher, eg: Socretes, Plato. The influence of the individual philosophers started after the Renaissance. During the period of Renaissance, a large number of books prescribed and developed by Arab Scholars were acquired by the European scholars. They travelled to the Eastern centres of knowledge and collected informations as much as possible. The real individual influence on each started with John Amos Comenius, who was a Christian priest. He is called the 'Father of Modern Education'.

John Amos Comenius (1592 – 1670)

Comenius was born in Amsterdam, Czech Republic. An educational reformer and religious leader, he is remembered mainly for his innovations in methods of teaching; especially, languages. His main books are 'Janua Linguarum Rescrate' (Gate of Tongues unlocked) and 'The school of Infancy' that deals with language learning. He read with enthusiasm the works of Francis Bacon. He tried to rebuild society through a reformed educational system. He advocated full-time schooling for all the youths of the nation and they should be taught both their native culture and culture of Europe. He was best known for his original contributions to educational technique.

Comenius is chiefly known as an educationist as well as social reformer. Men all over Europe had looked to him as a leader, his vision had impressed many. His dream of universal harmony was too vague and too grandiose for the mental outlook of 17th century, which was already in a utilitarian and materialistic direction; it has had even less appeal in modern times. He believed profoundly in the unity of mankind.

In his view a revolution in methods of teaching was necessary so that learning might become rapid, pleasant and thorough. Teachers ought to 'follow in the footsteps of nature'. They ought to pay attention to the mind of the child and to the way the student learned. He suggested a better way of teaching Latin than the inefficient and the pedantic methods then in use. He advocated 'nature's way'; learning about things and not about grammar.

Comenius turned to the reform of human society through education. He accepted an offer from Government of Sweden to help reform its schools by writing a series of text books. He tried to lay a philosophical foundation for a science of pedagogy. He put forward certain self evident principles from which he derived a number of maxims, some of them full of commonsense. His chief attention was directed to his system of 'pansophy'. He believed that men could be trained to see the underlying harmony of the universe and thus to overcome its apparent disharmony. He advocated that everything might be pleasurable in itself and necessary for the expanding of the appetite of child.

Comenius is chiefly known as an educationist as well as social reformer. His ideas on curriculum content and teaching were much ahead of his time. He advocated a wider curriculum and saw it as a means to achieve universal brotherhood. The methods he proposed were gentler and more considerate of the child than were typical in his day and he suggested basic teaching on the concrete experiences of the child.

He favoured broad general education, rather than the narrow training of his day, which emphasized the study of languages. He urged the establishment of more schools and universities. Comenius was one of the first authors who believed that children's books should entertain as well as teach. His text book *Orbis Sensualium Pictus* (Visible world) was the first children's book in which illustrations played a major part. He stated that he wanted to attract the readers' attention 'with pictures that amusingly teach the chief things of this world'.

Education according to Comenius is not merely the training of the child at school or in the home, it is a process affecting man's whole life and the countless social adjustments he must make. The central idea is probably that of nature as a creator of forms. He encountered as a language teacher and organiser of schools, managed to achieve an inner unity, finding it in the elaborations of philosophy based on education. Comenius' genius lay in grasping the fact that education is nature's formative machinery and so integrating the educative process into a system in which this process is indeed the essential axis. Comenius may undoubtedly be considered as one of the precursors of the genetic idea in developmental psychology, and as the founder of a system of progressive instructions adjusted to the stage of development the pupil has reached. He distinguishes four major periods or stages in education: infancy, childhood, adolescense and youth. Comenius presents the following proposition regarding these successive stages, which shows deep psychological understanding. 'Though these schools be different, we do not wish them to teach different things, but rather the same things in a different manner. I mean, all things which can make men truly men, and the learned truly learned; they should be taught in considerations of pupils' age and the standard of his prior preparation, which should always tend gradually upward'. On school teaching he remarks three rules which derives the idea of spontaneous development of children.

1. If the class room instruction be curtailed as much as possible, namely to four hours, and if the same length of time be left for personal study.
2. If the pupil be forced to memorise as little as possible, that is to say, only the important things; of the rest they need only grasp the general meaning.
3. If everything be arranged to suit the capacity of the pupil, which increases naturally with study and age.

He introduced and dominated the whole modern movement in the field of science education. He is for Education as Newton for science. There are few problems in education that are not discussed by him. The most outstanding work is the 'Great Didact' originally written in Czech language and later in Latin and translated in to English in 1896. Comenius was interested in discovering method of teaching. The duty of the teachers of the young is to skillfully scatter the seeds of instruction int their minds'. 'As soon as once we find out the carrier method very easy to adopt, then method may be adopted. It is now quite clear that order which is the dominating principle can be borrowed from the operation of the nature. If we take nature as our guide, she will never lead us astray. Those things that placed before the intelligence of the young must be real things, not the shadow of things, as far as possible, be placed before senses. If the objects can not be procured, representation may be used. Copies or models may be constructed. The same principle be adopted by botanist, geometricians, Zoologists and geographers, who should illustrate the description by engravings by the object described.

'What has to be done must be learnt by practice in schools, therefore let the students learn to write by writing, to talk by talking, to sing by singing, to reason by reasoning. In this way, schools will become workshops humming with work. The student should first examine this model and initiate'.

The use of instrument should be shown in practice and not by words, ie. by example rather than by percepts.

The proper education of the young does not consist in stuffing their heads with words, sentences and ideas dragged together out of various authors, but in opening their understanding to the outer world. So that a stream may flow from their own.

Pedagogic Principles

He believed in some basic pedagogic principles. Some of them are:

- Teachers' duty is to water God's plants. The difference between the teachers and others is like the trained and un-trained gradeners.
- Teacher has to watch the operations of nature and carefully initiate them in teaching.
- Teacher's task is to present 'things' (real objects) that make an impression on their 'Scinsco' and imagination. Methods of sensuous perception will lead to the permanent retention of knowledge. Seeing is better than Learning.
- Pupils should be taught to learn by practice. Let them learn to write by writing, talk by talking etc.
- A definite model of what is to be learnt must be provided by the teachers. The use of instruments should be shown in practice, by example rather than by precepts. Rules are like thorns to the understanding-no one has mastered any language or and by precepts.
- Teachers should not stuff the young heads with information. Take pains to open the fountain of knowledge hidden in the scholars.

The result is that most men possess no information, but quotations, sentences etc. (Men must learn the world of objects, not books)

- Students should be allowed to advance slowly. They should not be forced to have six to eight hours instruction. The ease and pleasant areas of study is to be increased.
- Comenius advised for motivating children to participate in the teaching-learning process.
- He did not agree with giving severe punishment, 'we must take great care, not to use these extreme measures too readily'.
- The desire to know and to learn should be excited in boys in every possible manner.
- The method of instruction should lighten the drudgery of learning. The school itself must be a pleasant place.

Jean Jacques Rousseau (1712-1778)

Rousseau was born in Geneva, Switzerland in 1712. He was a French philosopher, the most important writer of the *Age of Reason*. His political philosophy influenced the development of French revolution; his theories have great impact on education and literature as well as on political philosophy. He attacked the traditional Christain doctrines of education in his book 'Emile'. He criticised the then existing society. His book 'Social contract' is a land mark in the history of political science.

Rousseau believed that man is not a social being by nature. He felt that when men lived in a state of nature, isolated and without language, they were good-they had no motive or impulse to hurt one another. But as soon as men began to live together in society, they became evil. According to him, society corrupts men by bringing out their inclinations towards aggression and wrong-doings. He believed that society should be reorganized into communities in which all persons would be completely controlled. He did not advise that men returns to a state of nature. He wanted a single agricultural society, in which men's desire controlled and all their energies directed toward total involvement in community.

Rousseau had his own views of education. He recommended the plan of a new education as the necessary preparation for a new way of understanding life. What he attempted was not any improvement in the existing method, but a complete revolution of established theories about the aims, as well as the methods, of a rational education with the object of attaining a new goal.

The full and healthy development of the 'natural man' is the purpose of education; not mean the man possessing of special learning; but the man best prepared to meet and master the ordinary conditions and accidents of life. The principal rule of Rousseau is the just purpose of education is not to impart learning, but to develop natural faculties by suitable exercise. A well developed man is fully prepared for the conditions and accidents of human life. Accepting education, however, in this sense, is the development of natural faculties, and the entrance in to the full possession of human life. We have to recognize that the role played in this education by parents and teachers is comparatively limited. Each one of us undergoes three kinds of education. First of all there is the education of nature through the development of our bodily, mental and moral faculties. Secondly, there is the education of things, the lessons of experience and the influence of external surroundings. And thirdly, there is the education we receive from our fellow beings, either deliberately bestowed upon us as instructions and counsels, or unconsciously imposed upon us by force or examples.

By the destruction of traditionalism, Rousseau brought education into closer relations with human welfare and opened the way to numerous social movements in modern education. By his rejection of books and the experience of the past, in favour of native and observational work, Rousseau helped develop the use of science in the curriculum.

In his most revolutionary treatise on education, the 'Emile', he undertook to show how education might minimize the drawbacks of civilization and bring man as near to nature as possible. In 'Emile' it is also aimed to replace the conventional and formal education of the day with a training that should be natural and spontaneous. His basic principle is that 'everything is good as it comes from the hands of the 'author of Nature'; but everything degenerates in the hands of man'. According to him men are educated by 'three kinds of teachers – nature, man and things, and since the co-operation of the three education is necessary for their perfection, it is to the one over which we have no control (ie. nature) that we must direct the other two'.

Rousseau recommends the education consisted of physical activities, in the first period. In the next stage, considerations to sense training, although incidentally he is given same idea of conduct and property.

In order to learn to think, we must then exercise our limbs, senses and our organs which are the instruments of our intelligence. In the third phase, instruction in the natural sciences through curiosity and interest in investigation may be given. In the fourth, moral training through contact with the unfortunate and the criminal elements of society, is important. At the fifth stage he gives importance to women's education. The whole education of women ought to be relative to men. To please them, to be useful them, to educate them when young, to case for them when grown, to counsel them, to console them, to make life agreeable and sweet to them. There are the duties of women at all times, and what should be taught then form infancy'.

A man's happiness and virtue are in the right use of his liberty; there is not virtue without effort, the word virtue means essential force. Virtue can belong only to an imperfect being weak by his infirmity, strong by his will, inspired by the love of goodness. If the spirit of man was compelled to follow virtue, what merit would belong to him for taking his appointed place, in a pre-established order he had neither wish nor motive for troubling?. He would lack the moral enjoyment, that love of virtue brings; he would lack the noble interest; he would lose the satisfaction of success. He would be perfect, as the angles are; but no doubt a virtuous man is worth more. The supreme happiness for man is in the contentment that follows voluntary obediense to the inner law. To deserve this contentment he exists on the earth evolved with free choice, tempted by his passions, retrained by conscience.

The plan of a new education is for to the necessary preparation for a new way of understanding life. What he attempted was not any improvement in the existing method, but a complete revolution of established theories about the aims, as well as the methods, of a rational education with the object of attaining a new goal.

The full and healthy development of the 'natural man' is the purpose of education; and again the 'well-educated man' does not mean the man possessed of special learning; but the man best prepared to meet and master the ordinary conditions and accidents of life. The principal rule of Rousseau is the just purpose of education is not to impart learning, but to develop natural faculties by suitable exercise. To him a well-developed man is fully prepared for the conditions and accidents of human life. In the natural order of things the universal vocation is the human state: who so is well educated for that can not fill badly any of those conditions that it includes. Before the vocation chosen for the child by his parents, Nature has called him to human life. 'To live is the trade I would teach my pupil. Upon leaving my hands, he will not be a soldier, a lawyer, nor a priest: but, if I am successful, he will deserve first of all to be called a man; and hence all that a man can and should be or do-he will, at need, be able to fit himself for, as well as my other.' Accepting education, however, in this sense as the development of natural faculties, and the entrance into the full possession of human life, we have to recognize that the share taken in this education by parents and teachers is comparatively limited and if a helpful, a subordinate share.

Rousseau contended that man is essentially good, a 'noble savage' 'when in the state of nature' and that good people are made unhappy and corrupted by their experiences in society. He viewed society as 'artificial' and 'corrupt' and that the furthering of society results in the continuing unhappiness of man. In his essay, 'Discourse on the Arts and Science', he argued that the advancement of art and science had not been beneficial to mankind. He proposed that the progress of knowledge had made government more powerful, and crushed individual liberty. He concluded that material progress had actually undermined the possibility of sincere friendship, replaying, it with jealousy, fear and suspicion. In his most important work 'The social contract', he describes the relationship of man with society. Contrary to his earlier work, Rousseau claimed that the state of nature is brutish condition without law or morality and that there are good men only as a result of societies and that there are good men only as the result of society's presence. In the state of nature man is prone to be in frequent competition with his fellow men. Because he can be successful facing threats by joining with other men, he has the impetus to do so. He joins together with his fellow men to form the collective human presence known as 'society'. The 'Social Contract' is the 'compact' agreed to among men that sets the condition for membership in society.

Rousseau was one of the first modern writers to seriously attack the institution of private property, and therefore is considered a forebear of modern socialism and communism. Rousseau also questioned the assumption that the will of the majority is always correct. He argued the goal of government should be to secure freedom, equality and justice for all within the state, regardless of the will of the majority.

Philosophy in brief

1. Material world is the real world
2. Mind is subordinate to matter
3. Nature alone is the source of all knowledge
4. Values are created in terms of specific needs
5. All real values exist in nature in living close to nature
6. There is no possibility of any 'supernatural being'
7. The individual is always given precedence
8. Man creates societies only to meet some of his needs

Principles of Education

1. Rousseau lays stress on physical environment
2. He emphasizes the present life of the child as the basis of education
3. He accords an important place to the child in the educative process
4. He advocates education in accordance with the nature of child
5. He gives prominent place to the concept of freedom in the education of the child
6. He gives an insignificant place for knowledge from books or bookish knowledge
7. He regards education as the dynamic side of philosophy

Aims of Education

According to Rousseau, the main aims of education are self expression, autonomous development of individuality, improvement of racial gains, preparation for the struggle for existence etc. The curriculum should be based on the nature and interest of the child. It lays stress on subjects helpful to self-preservation. Basic science, physical and health education may also be given importance in the curriculum. Rousseau recommends learning by doing, learning through experience, observation and through heuristic methods – as the chief methods of teaching – learning process. He suggests the role of the teacher as an observer and stage – setter. He is the apostle of child – centered education. His remarks on teaching: 'I do not like verbal explanations. Young people pay little heed to them nor do they remember them. We lay too much stress upon words. We teachers babble and our scholars follow our example. Never tell the child what he cannot understand, no descriptions, no eloquence'. Rousseau is the apostle of child-centred education. "Thus, education was to be for Rousseau the art of managing opposites with an eye to the development of a truly autonomous or self-reliant freedom". 'It is therefore important to organize the transmission of knowledge in such a way that the child takes the task upon itself'.

John Dewey (1859-1952)

John Dewey was an American philosopher and educator and one of the founders of the philosophical school of 'Pragmatism'. He was known as a pioneer of functional psychology and a leader of progressive movement in education in U.S.A. He eagerly embraced the views of 19th century German philosopher Hegel, who gave emphasis to the spiritual and organic nature of the universe. The search for a philosophy of education became a major concern for Dewey and added a new dimension to his thinking. He preferred scientific investigation mode of inquiry. He developed a philosophical ground for democracy and liberalism. "He conceived democracy as a mode of association which provides the members of a society with the opportunity for maximum experimentation and personal growth"[(9)].

In formulating educational criteria and aims, he drew heavily on the insights into learning. He viewed thought and learning as a process of inquiry starting from doubt or uncertainty and spurred by desire to resolve practical frictions or relieve strain and tension. Education, must therefore begin with experience, which has at its aim growth and achievement of maturity. The educational process must begin with the build upon interests of the child; that it must provide opportunity for the interplay of thinking and doing in the child's classroom experience; that the teacher should be a guide and co-worker with the pupils, rather than a task master, and that school's goal is the growth of the child in all aspects of its being. His book 'Experience and Nature' (1925) includes the most important aspects of his philosophy and generally regarded as his 'magnum opus'. His thought covered a wide range of topics and theory of knowledge, psychology, education, social philosophy, fine arts and religion. He became the foremost philosopher and one of the most productive scholars of his nation. Some of his other remarkable works are:

'The School and Society' (1900), 'Democracy and Education' (1916), 'Philosophy and Civilization', 'Experience and Education' 91938), 'Freedom and Culture' (1939), 'Education Today' (1949), 'Philosophy of Education', 'Dewey on Education' (1959) etc.

Dewey's ideas and proposals strongly affected educational theory and practice. He had forty seven years of teaching careers at Columbia University and became the most widely known and influential teacher in America. His thought covered a wide range of topics including logic and theory of knowledge, psychology, education, social philosophy, fine arts and religion. He became the foremost philosopher and one of the nation's most productive scholars.

His philosophy is termed as 'Experimentalism, Functionalism, Instrumentation, Operationalism, Progressism, Practicalism, and pragmatism as its emphasis was on dynamic and ever changing character of life. He does not believe in any absolute values or ultimate moral principles. Utility is the touchstone of every value, what works in a practical situation is true, what does not work is false, truth is not a fixed or eternal thing, but is subject to change. what is true today may be false tomorrow.

Dewey stressed the values:

1. Aesthetic taste or capacity
2. Conscientiousness
3. Efficiency
4. Scientific spirit
5. Sociability and social efficiency

Experience and Experimental Methods

Where there is experience, there is living. To learn from experience is to make a connection between what we do to things and what we enjoy or suffer from things. Experiences cannot be educative; education is development within, by, and for experience.. Education by, of , and for experience is constant revision on the work of experimental inquiry.

Dewey is of the concept of education as growth and direction. Life is growing and education is the process for this ever-increasing growth. Dewey thinks on the process of adjustment. Prof. Dewey states in "The School and Society", "what the best and wisest parent thinks for his own child that the community want for all of its children". He believes that the only true education comes through the stimulation of the childs' powers by the demands of the social situation in which he finds himself.

Philosophical ideas

Dewey recommended the philosophical movement-'Pragmatism'. He is strongly influenced by science of psychology and by the theory of evolution by the English scientist-Charles R. Darwin. He regarded intelligence as a power that man uses when he faces a conflict or challenges.

According to him man lives by customs and habit. In certain situation new response is needed to respond to the problem. Man can not solve such problems by habitual action and thought. He must use intelligence as an instrument for overcoming the obstacles. This philosophy of Dewey is called 'instrumentalism'.

He believed that knowledge is a means of controlling the environment, to improve the quality of human life.

He focussed on how to close the gap between thought and action. This interpretation of science shows how thought and action are limited.

He considered science as a method for inquiring into the behaviour of things. The results of such inquiry are the joint products of thought and activity. Dewey regarded activity as conducting experiments under controlled situation and thought as those theories that guide our experiments.

A detailed genetic analysis of the process of inquiry was Dewey's signal contribution to studies. Dewey distinguished three phases of the process. It begins with the problematic situation, a situation where instinctive or habitual responses of the human organism to the environment are inadequate for the continuation of ongoing activity in pursuit of the fulfillment of needs and desires. Dewey stressed in studies and subsequent writings that the uncertainty of the problematic situation is not inherently cognitive, but practical and existential. Cognitive elements enter into the process as a response to precognitive maladjustment. Moral and social problems are concerned with the guidance of human action to the achievement of socially defined ends that are productive of a satisfying life for individuals within the social context. Dewey, throughout his ethical and social writings, stressed the need for an open-ended flexible, and experimental approach to problems of practice aimed at the determination of the conditions for the attainment of human goods and a critical examination of the consequences of means adopted to promote them, an approach that he called the 'method of intelligence'.

Curriculum

Dewey advocates broader curricular programmes and emphasizes the total development of the person for the task of educating so many children at so many different educational levels with such a variety of abilities, needs and goods etc. Social life cannot be cut into pieces of knowledge. Departmentalization of the curriculum and the systematic succession of studies have to be replaced by an elastic programme of activities.

Methods of teaching

The teacher is a guide and director; he steers the boat, but the energy that propels it must come from those who are learning. The more a teacher is aware of the past experiences of students, of their hopes, desires, chief interests, the better will he understand the forces at work that need to be directed and utilized for the formation of reflective habits. "Teacher is the prophet of the true God. The teacher is engaged into simply in the training of individuals, but in the formation of the proper social life[(10)]". Dewey's method of teaching is of pragmatic attitude which consists in looking away from first things, principles, and of looking towards last things, fruits, consequences, facts. It is therefore, in submitting conceptions to the control of experience, in the process of verifying them, that one finds examples of what is called truth. Truth means verification.

Dewey's contributions to educational thought and practice

1. His theory of education, coupled with the logic of experimental method has been very influential in the development of modern education practices.

2. The greatest change has been in the recognition of the worth of the experiences of the child. The child is no longer regarded as a passive subject meant for the imposition of external information but is considered an active living being whose interests have to be stimulated by participation in socially significant experiences. This kind of participation is a kind of moral experience. It is essential to stress the meaningful dimensions of the process of learning.

3. He has tried to introduce a more human touch in the process of education.

4. He has interpreted the school as a community for the realization of the significance of the immediate experiences and present opportunities of the child if he is to be a contributor to the march of the social process.

5. His insistence on activity of diverse kinds in schools is also another aspect of his social theory of education.

6. The pragmatic method of instrumentalistic experimentation reacts against all kinds of mysticism, transcendentalism and absolutism.

7. The supreme contribution of Dewey to a philosophy of education is the theory of scientific democratic humanism.

8. Dewey is quite right in pleading for the wide use of the experimental methods of science in education.

As an educator, he opposed the traditional method of learning by memory under the authority of teachers. He believed that education should not be concerned only with the mind. Students should develop manual skills. Learning must be related to the interest of students and connected with current problems. Education must include a students' physical and moral well-being as well as his intellectual development.

John Dewey regarded education as incomplete if it ignores the daily experiences of its seeker.

REFERENCES

1. Al-Ghazzali's *Ihya Ulum-id-din*. Translation by Maulana Fazl al-Karim. Darul Ifta, Egypt, p.11.
2. *The Concise Encyclopaedia of Islam*. Vol. 1. Oxford, London, p. 138.
3. Al-Ghazzali's *Ihya Ulum-id-din*. Translation by Maulana Fazl al-Karim. Darul Ifta, Egypt, p. 28.
4. Al-Hadith.
5. Shaikh, M. Sa'eed, *Studies in Muslim Philosophy*. Adam Publishers, New Delhi, p.182.
6. Ibid, p.195.
7. Rosenthal, Franz, *Ibn Khaldun, Muqaddimah*. Oxford, London, p.481.
8. Sarton, George, *Introduction to the History of Science*. Carnegie Institute, London, p.217.
9. The New Encyclopaedia Britanica Vol. 4., Oxford, London, p.52.
10. Ibid, p.173.

DESIGN OF THE STUDY

CHAPTER IV

DESIGN OF THE STUDY

- Method of Study
- Sources of Data
- Primary Sources
- Secondary Sources
- Analysis

DESIGN OF THE STUDY

Research is considered to be the more formal, systematic and intensive process of carrying on a scientific method of analysis, which is directed toward discovery and development of an organized body of knowledge. It is defined as the systematic and objective analysis and recording of controlled observations that may lead to the development of generalizations, principles or theories resulting in prediction and possibly ultimate control of events. "Historical research describes the process involved in investigating, recording, analyzing and interpreting the events of the past for the purpose of making generalizations that are helpful in understanding the past and the present and to a limited extent, in anticipating the future"(1).

Method of the study

The investigator has adopted the method of historical analysis as the most suitable method to carry out this study. The content for analysis of the study is mainly related to the past history of Islamic education with special reference to Islamic philosophy and its influence on the present system of education.

The underlying assumption of the present study are that theory and practice of education has been directly or indirectly influenced by the

Islamic philosophy of education. Besides, it has also been assumed that the modern concepts of education have a positive direct or indirect relationship with the Islamic concepts of education.

Sources of Data

The information for the study has been collected by referring to many volumes of books and authoritative publications written by eminent scholars as the subject has a wide coverage. Also the information has been collected from different other sources by means of reference, interviews and consultations. They were systematically codified organised and analysed. The investigator relied mainly on two categories of sources for collecting the data, viz. Primary sources and Secondary sources.

Primary sources

"The original documents or remains which are the first witness of a fact are termed as primary sources"(2). Primary sources are considered to be original because they are authoritative evidences as far as the subject of the study is concerned. They are sources which form solid basis for the study and provides dependable information that cannot be found anywhereelse and enables the investigator to make valid judgements on the subject of the study.

1. As far as the present study is concerned the Holy Qur'an, which is the basis of Islamic philosophy, is the most important primary source. The

authority of Holy Qur'an, as primary source is universally accepted. Therefore its authenticity need not be established by means of external or internal criticism. According to Islam, the Qur'an is the collection of divine messages revealed to Prophet Muhammed on several occasions within a span of 23 years of his prophethood (from AD 611 to 634). According to Islam it is Allah's eternal miracle revealed to Prophet Muhammed and through him to all succeeding generations. It contains a complete code which provides for all areas of life, whether spiritual, intellectual, political, social or economic. It is a code which has no boundaries of time, place or nation. It is a guidance to the whole of mankind.

All the Surahs (chapters) of the Qur'an had been recorded in writing before the prophet's death and many Muslims had committed the whole Qur'an to memory. So well it has been preserved both in memory and in writing, that the Arabic Text we have today is identical to the text which was revealed to the Prophet. Not even a single letter has yielded to corruption during the passage of centuries.

Allah has perfected his religion for all mankind with regulation of this Book. "This day have I perfected your religion for you, completed My favour upon you, I have chosen for you Islam as your religion"(3). Qur'anic verses encompass knowledge in the areas of philosophy, history, economics, jurisprudence and several other sciences.

2. Another primary source depended on for this study is Hadith. Hadith is the collection of sayings of Prophet Muhammed compiled by the approved authors ie: the reporters of which, there is no doubt on their piety and truthfulness Such Hadith are called "Sahih" ie: accurate. The Hadiths are treated as having the second place to that of the Holy Qur'an in the Islamic Sharia'th. Hence there is no need of establishing the authenticity of the sayings of the Prophet, as far as 'Sahih' Hadiths are concerned. Most of these Hadiths are reported by the six renowned reporters, known as 'Sihahu sithath', ie: Bukhari, Muslim, Abu-Davud, Thirmudi, Ibn Majah and Nasa'i.

3. There is a huge body of literature including articles, treatises, interpretations of eminent scholars and Islamic experts which can be depended on as primary source for the study. However their authenticity is to be established by external or internal criticism as the case may be.

Secondary Sources

"Secondary sources are the reports of a person who relates the testimony of an actual witness of, or participant in an event, the writer of the secondary source was not on the scene of the event, but merely reports what person who was there said or wrote"(4). For a good research project it is necessary for the researcher to collect the data from as many primary sources as possible. Secondary sources sometimes prove very useful in providing information about primary sources. 'The writer of the secondary source was not on the scene of the event but merely report what the person who was present there said or wrote'.

In secondary sources, the investigator complies and summarises the findings of the work done by others and gives interpretations to these findings. He usually attempts to cover all the important studies in an area in the form of encyclopaedia of education, education indexes, abstracts, bibliographies, bibliographical references as sources of quotation. This type of wide reference is done inorder to collect an elaborated awareness on the particular areas and to develop a critical outlook on each side of the subject matter and to collect necessary questions and connected items for establishing the most authenticated facts.

The secondary sources useful for the investigator are plenty. A large number of secondary sources are collected from many centres and institutions. The investigator's association with several centres of Islamic learning is South India helped him to collect the necessary information in abundance.

As far as the present study is concerned the following important documents have been relied on as secondary sources:

1. Al – Ghazzali's 'Ihya Uloomiddin', translation by Maulana Fazl al Karim. Egypt. 1933.
2. 'Curriculum and Teacher Education', Mohammed al-Afendi, King Abdul Aziz University, Jeddah, 1980.

3. The Life of Muhammed, Haykal, Delhi, 1990.
4. History of the Arabs by P.K. Hitti, Oxford University Press, London, 1937.
5. The Oxford History of Islam – by Oxford University Press, Cambridge, 1984.
6. The Islamic Encyclopaeida (Mal.), Islamic Publishing House, Calicut, 2000.
7. The contributions of Arabs to Education, Totah K.A., New York, 1926.
8. 'Educational Philosophy of Holy Qur'an' by Dr. Mahar Abdul Haq, New Delhi, 1991.
9. Ibn Khaldun's Muqaddimah by Franz Rosenthal (English Translation), London, 1967.
10. 'Aims and Objectives of Islamic Education' by Syed Muhammed Al-Naqib etc., New Delhi, 1979.

As a basis for analysis, formative study of philosophers of modern education and educational views of Islamic scholars have been made use of.

Analysis

Based on the information gathered from the primary and secondary sources, the investigator used the technique of verbal analysis and interpretations to substantiate the hypotheses formed. The influence of

Islamic philosophy on the following areas of educational theory and practice is highlighted in the final analysis.

1. Aims and Objectives
2. Curriculum structure
3. Curriculum transaction
4. Teacher-pupil relationship
5. Educational management etc.

In the present study a combination of historical and analytical methods based on intensive study of primary and secondary sources is employed. Related books and documents on Islamic modern philosophical views on education and other publications on the subject have also been made use of.

REFERENCES

1. Best, John. W., *Research in Education*, New Delhi, Printice Hall of India, 1992, p.74.

2. Sukhia S.P., Mehrothra P.V. and Mehrothra R.N. *Elements of Educational Research*, Allied publishers Bombay, 1974.

3. Ali, Abdullah Yusuf, *Holy Qur'an*, 05:03, Beirut, 1987.

4. Best, John W., *Research in Education*, Printice Hall of India, 1992, p.66.

CRITICAL ANALYSIS

CHAPTER V

CRITICAL ANALYSIS

1. Islamic Philosophy in brief
    - Nature of man and his place in the world.
    - Nature of knowledge
    - Nature of values
2. The Islamic System of Education: Characteristics
    - Aims and objectives of Islamic Education
    - Curriculum Development
    - Curriculum Transaction
    - Teacher-Pupil Interaction
    - Educational Management
    - The Mosques
    - The Madrasah System
3. Islamic Philosophy: Its Influence on Modern Education
    - Aims and Objectives
    - Curriculum Development
    - Curriculum Transaction
    - Teacher-Pupil Interaction
    - Educational Management
4. Influence of Islamic knowledge on the West

CRITICAL ANALYSIS

A critical study of the factors of Islamic philosophy which must have exerted its influence on education is attempted in this chapter with a view to verifying the hypotheses formed. It is intended to make a detailed discussion on each of the hypotheses.

1. Islamic Philosophy in brief

The 'philosophy' which teaches the various aspects of philosophy in Islamic perspective is termed as 'Islamic Philosophy'. The very word 'philosophy' has its origin in the Arabic word 'Falsafah'. The Arab Muslims and other dignitories from various countries contributed a lot to the science of philosophy. The Islamic philosophy deals with the relation of man with God and man with man and other living and non-living beings in the universe. It demands the man for the service of God, it is the highest articulation of learning and it can be attained through the service of the humanity as a whole. Islamic philosophy proposes the creation of a new generation of young men and women who will not lose touch with their own tradition or who are not unaware of developments in any branch of human knowledge. The fundamental principles of Islamic philosophy are to develop in man a living sense of God both in thought and action and equip how to work for a life of peace, in order that mankind might live together as a 'family of God'.

Qura'n and Sunnah are the fundamental bases of Islamic Philosophy. Qura'n is the literal words of Allah, revealed by Him to Prophet Muhammed during twenty three years of his Prophethood through the Angel 'Jibreel'. They were memorized by Muhammed, who dictated them to his companions when in turn memorized them, wrote down, and reviewed them with Prophet Muhammed. More over Prophet Muhammed reviewed the Qura'n with the Angel 'Jibreel' once in every Ramadan and twice in the last year of his life time. Since the Qur'an was revealed, there has always been a large number of Muslims who have memorized all of the Qur'an, letter by letter. Some of them have been able to memorize all of the Qur'an by the age of ten. Thus, it is not surprising to note that even a single letter of the Qur'an has not been changed till date.

The Qur'an, which was revealed fourteen centuries ago, contain divine statements of certain facts that were recently discovered by scientist. This proves without doubt that the Qur'an must be literal words of Allah, revealed by Him to Prophet Muhammed, and also that Muhammed, is truly a messenger and Prophet sent by Allah. It is beyond doubt that any one fourteen hundred years ago would have known such scientific facts which have been discovered or proven true very recently with the help of advanced equipments and sophisticated methods.

The Qur'an is, primarily and essentially, a book of guidance, including the basis of a code of life for mankind and was sent down to enable mankind to differentiate between right and wrong. "The Qura'n is not a book of science but it has references to many scientific things, which came to be explored scientifically much later than when they appeared in the Qura'nic revelations. In this way scientific explorations only help to establish the truth of the Qura'n as the word of God, that is unchangeable whereas scientific phenomena and the understanding of them are open to review and revision".[1]

'Sunnah' means the whole life of Prophet Muhammad especially from prophethood at the age of forty onwards. And it is the sayings of the Prophet (Ahadith), his model actions and his approvals as the guidelines, directions and solutions to various problems in all walks of life.

All the living-beings in the universe are the creations of Almighty Allah. According to Qura'n, Allah exists and is one, and that He is the Creator, the Master, the Provider, the Sustainer, the Ultimate metaphysical cause, purpose and end of everything. Qur'an declares ": He is Allah, The One; Allah, the Eternal, Absolute".[2] Man is placed by Him as the most superior to all other creations. Islam proclaims the uniqueness of man and the uniqueness and beauty of the universe. It is a part of the great design of the Master-mind. Islam considers life in this world as a means of achieving happiness in the hereafter whereas many of the modern philosophers consider life in this world as its final goal.

For worship the Holy Qur'an uses the word 'Ibadat'. 'Ibadat' is :

- something done with a relish, hence it is a work of devotion, love, fervour and a sincerity of the heart;
- something that is certainly beneficial not only physically but also spiritually, giving full satisfaction to the mind;
- something that entails a little bit of hardship also, though this hardship is beneficial to him who undergoes it.

The daily prayers as a form of necessary and compulsory discipline and an effective practical training of equality. The prescribed five times' daily prayers provide the most effective training in democracy. Equality before Allah five times a day is reflected as equality among men for the rest of the time also. The rich and the poor, the high and the low, the powerful and the weak, the young and the old, the ruler and the ruled all stand shoulder to shoulder and all humble themselves equally together before Allah.

A person offering his prayers dutifully at different hours spread over the day and a part of the night, remains always necessarily clean in body and dress. Washing the usually exposed parts of the body keeps one fresh all the day long. Being no priesthood is allowed in Islam, the best man in respect of knowledge and piety in the congregation has to lead the prayers. Once a leader is chosen, he is strictly obeyed in all the movements. This is another form of training in democracy, leadership and discipline. All Muslims living on the earth turn their faces towards one symbolic centre of unity and fraternity. This strengthens the belief in the unity of Allah, the unity of mankind and the unity of faith in a universal nationality. Prayer itself is not an end, but a means to achieve spiritual uplift of the individual as well as the society. It improves a person's social morality and discipline in democratic way.

The Muslim Ummah is ideally a classless society. Every member of the society must have the competency to earn his living. Even the Caliphs and Governors have no exception to it. They may draw their salary from the treasury to the extent to which it suffices to their bare needs of life. All jobs carry equal status. All members of the society are workmen and can be called to do any hard manual work any time by the Ummah. So vocational training is compulsory for all. Every one must get according to his needs and the surplus wealth must always remain in circulation. Superiority or inferiority in jobs or gradation thereof on any basis other than righteousness is against the Qur'anic injunctions. Every work is labour and every labour is dignified. Performing duty honestly is worship.

Nature of man and his place in the world

Man is sent as the Vicegerent of God to earth. "Behold, your Lord said to the angels; 'I will create a vicegerent on earth.'"[(3)] Man is made superior to all other beings and is endowed with qualities, which differentiate him from other creations. He is created for and sent to the universe, which is very unique in nature. All the things in the nature are created for the well-being of the mankind. Man is created for worshiping the God; and thereby serving the mankind. Man is the part of the society and he is entrusted to maintain and uphold its progress alongwith ensuring the all-round development of his individuality. The Islamic view of the uniqueness of the nature of the universe is in agreement with the statements of modern philosophers and their educational thoughts. This stream of thought that is the uniqueness of man and nature, can be found generally in the works of all modern educational philosophers, particularly in the educational philosophy of Rousseau, eventhough he was not a believer in religion.

Islam considers a child innocent and righteous when he is born. God has mentioned man as His best creation in the Universe. He has endowed man with intelligence and knowledge. So, man is treated as more accountable and answerable to God than any other beings, to each of his thoughts, words and actions. Islam admits no discrimination among men on the basis of race, creed, colour, nation or anything else except their piety and righteousness. "Islamic philosophy prepares man to assume the responsibilities of the highest creation of God as His vicegerent. Naturally he should develop the qualities of high character and should prepare to occupy the seat of high rank. Verily the most honoured of you in the sight of Allah is (he who is) the most righteous of you"[(4)].

Nature of Knowledge

Islam gave immense importance to knowledge and acquisition of knowledge. "Acquisition of knowledge is incumbent upon all the faithful men and women" [(5)]. Every Muslim is bound to acquire knowledge till his death. Islam advocates unity of knowledge and universality of education. So it is not in favour of dividing knowledge as 'material' and 'spiritual'. Moreover, Islam recommends acquiring knowledge on contemporary worldly matters.

According to Islamic concept, the sources of knowledge is categorised into two. They are Divine revelation and Human intellect, which constantly interacts with universe by observation, contemplation, experimentation and application. Man cannot, by himself, be rightly guided to the Divine truth and life cannot be regulated in the proper manner in the absence of unchangeable injunctions inspired by Allah. Hence the need of Divine revelation. Knowledge is essential for maintaining the discipline that assures the recognition and acknowledgement of one's proper place in relation to one's self, society and community, one's proper place in relation to one's physical, intellectual and spiritual capacities and potentialities. However, knowledge is essential to understand the Divine injunctions. "And such are the parables We setforth for mankind. But only those who have knowledge understand them". [(6)]

Nature of Values

According to Islam, values have great importance. Islamic philosophy relies on certain eternal values. The worldly life here is a preparation for the eternal life in the hereafter. The Holy Qur'an instructs 'to make preparation for the eternal journey and the best of which is piety'. '... and take a provision (with you) for the journey, but the best of provision is right conduct. So fear Me, O ye that are wise'[(7)]. Prophet Muhammed instructed that a believer should live like a stranger or a traveller in this world; it indicates that the life in this world is transcendental. Islam considers spiritual values as the basis of life, but is against giving up the world and also against giving utmost importance to the worldly affairs. It recommends a middle, balanced path in between the two.

Each and every member of the society must always remain prepared to respond positively to the call of Allah and His Prophet. Members of the Muslim 'Ummah' (society) must not betray the trust in Allah and the Messenger. They must not misappropriate things entrusted to them. The Ummah's solidarity is based on union, mutual understanding and pure and sincere affection as he who enters the citadel of Islam, comes into the stronghold of universal fraternity and no power in the world can break this bond. Its source is Allah and nothing can be more valuable for a Muslim than Allah and His Messenger. 'The man must hold fast the rope of Allah under all circumstances and the Ummah must not be divided on any issue among themselves'. 'And hold fast, altogether, by the rope which Allah (stretches out for you), and be not divided among yourselves; ...' [8]. In Allah's Kingdom, the humble and the influential, the black and the white, the poor and the rich, the small and the big, all are treated with the same salutation and according to their degree of sincerity and submission to God.

The Qur'an, which is the basis of all values, demands the unity of mankind and respect for humanity and it is possible only when the men think in terms of oneness of its origin. The Holy Qur'an calls all the people of the world with its common message of the right path.

Islam gives importance to individual and society. It recommends the upliftment of the society by safeguarding the interest of the individual. Almost all actions in Islam justify this point. The five times daily prayers prescribed provide the most effective practical training on equality and they ensure the organized set up of the society and the spiritual purification of the individual, as well.

One of the hypotheses formed for this study has been that Islam has an independent philosophy which can be interpreted in terms of 'nature of man and his place in the world', 'nature of knowledge' and 'nature of values'. From the foregoing analysis, it has been found that the philosophy of Islam is a unique one which is rather different from other schools of philosophies as far as its views on 'nature of man and his place in the world' is concerned. Islamic philosophy has a firm epistemology which is based on divine revelation of knowledge. The source of knowledge according to Islam is Al-mighty God Himself. And Quran is the treasure of knowledge revealed to Prophet Muhammed and every branch of knowledge originates from God. Therefore Islam believes in the unity of knowledge. Code of values, therefore, is not decided by human beings nor formed by them. The values have been already prescribed by God and they were translated into his life by prophet Muhammed and his followers. One of the objectives of this study has been to understand the main characteristic features of Islamic philosophy. The analysis has clearly revealed the peculiar characteristics of Islamic Philosophy in terms of its conception of man, his nature and the epistemology and the axiology. Therefore the hypothesis No. 1 of this study that Islam has an independent Philosophy has been established. The fact that this philosophy has independent views on the 'nature of man and his place in the world' has also been substantiated. The views of Islamic Philosophy on the nature of knowledge and nature of values are rather based on Qur'an and Hadiths and there is no doubt that the Islamic Philosophy has an independent view of epistemology and axiology.

2. The Islamic System of Education: Characteristics

From the very beginning of Islam, there had been a particular system to educating the children. The mosques were the centres of education. The education was imparted free of cost. The pupils used to stay at the mosque, for educational training. They got training directly from the 'Usthad', (the teacher imparting religious education) theoretically and, to a certain extent, practically. The 'Usthad' used to teach his disciples at his house, which was usually built by the side of the mosque or as a part of it. So, the teacher could care each pupil individually and thereby the idea of 'case study' can be traced out at the Islamic system of education. The idea of free education of modern times has also its roots in the Islamic system of education in olden days. The spread of boarding schools has also the connection with the lodging arranged to the pupils in the madrassas, in the early Islamic system of education, which continues today also.

The main input in the Islamic system of education is considered as its pupils. So, the formation of good habits is to be ensured in all levels of education. The curriculum material must be suited to fulfil the above achievement. And at the same time, the teachers-the implementing agents of the curriculum-should also be the strict adherents of the above educational activities.

The output expected from the Islamic system of education is chiefly the pupils, who have undergone its process of study. The society will be benefited by the interaction of such refined and cultured personnels who will exhibit always good habits with sincere co-operation and committed dealings. The process of imparting the Islamic system of education must be based on God-fearing, sincerity and commitment. The curriculum and the contents consisted in it and the methodology of its transaction are to be in accordance with the objectives suited to Islamic education. A discussion in detail on this part will be coming in due course.

Education according to Islam, is a life-long process. Its aim should be to make the 'educant' perfect, pious and service-minded through the acquisition of knowledge and its application. By education Islam aims at the inculcation of right way of thinking and living, proper understanding of what constitutes human soul and moulding a healthy mind, giving the actual importance to worldly and spiritual matters.

The main aim of Islamic education is to understand the relation of man with God, man with man and man with nature etc. as revealed in the Holy Qur'an. The aim of Islamic education is the service to God, it is the highest articulation of learning and it can be attained through the service to the humanity as a whole. Education is the best means of creating a new generation of young men and women who will not lose touch with their own tradition or who are not unaware of developments in any branch of human knowledge. Education has been the most effective method of changing the attitudes of the young and thus leading to accept and initiate social change.

Aims and Objectives of Islamic education

Islamic education insists that piety and faith must clearly be recognized and attained individually. The aim of Islamic education is the creation of 'good and righteous man' who worships Allah in the true sense, builds up the structure of his earthly life according to the Sharia'h and employs it to subserve his faith. It aims at the balanced growth of the total personality of man through the training of his spirit, intellect and rational self-feelings and bodily senses. The ultimate aim of Islamic education lies in the realization of the complete submission of the individual, the community and the humanity at large to Allah. Islamic education builds in the minds of Muslim youth a resistance, an adaptability and a mechanism for adjustment in worldly matters other than the fundamental beliefs. An Islamic educational system can not be merely 'utilitarian' in character. It must teach the distinction between 'halal' (Permissible) and 'haram' (impermissible). It must instil the values of self-restraint.

On getting Islamic education the pupils are expected to be able to discharge the duty entrusted to them by the God, "Your are the best of peoples, evolved for mankind, enjoining what is right, forbidding what is wrong and believe in God".[9] Moreover they are directed to be witnesses and living examples of all the goodness on the earth, Qur'an says, "Thus we have made you a people justly balanced (of the middle path) so that you could be a witness (an example) to people and (just as) the Prophet is to you"[10]. Through the above Qur'anic verses, Muslims are directed to be the authorised life-witnesses of all the goodness and righteousness by right-thinking, words and actions. And they are instructed to be living model to all the human beings just as the Prophet Muhammed acted as a living example to them.

Islamic education aims to promote the awareness of God in the Universe. It has to start from an integrated system of education which will try to impart knowledge and information as well as values. An integrated system of education is wanted in which the study of the usual subjects which would not be viewed as discordant with the study of the Qur'an and so on. Education is a process that helps the balanced growth of the total personality of man. According to Islam, man is composed of spirit, soul and body. 'The Islamic system of education is so planned that the different branches of knowledge are considered as integrated units and not as completely independent items. One has to accept that man has a spirit and that spiritual and moral aspects of his personality cannot be separated from any form of human activity whether individual or social, i.e. human behaviour cannot be isolated and separated from its spiritual and moral components. Man is a spiritual being; he has a definite role to undertake in this world and his activities are governed by certain basic principles of conduct. "Let there arise out of you a band of people inviting to all that is good, enjoining what is right; and forbidding what is wrong; There are the ones to attain felicity"[(11)]. The Islamic concept is that of harmony between man and nature and not of confrontation. The Islamic concept is to know the basic laws of the universe in order to be able to control it and to use it for one's benefit without disturbing or corrupting external nature. All learning must re-order itself under the principle of 'Tawhid' ie: Allah exists and is one, and that He is the

Creator, the Master, Provider, Sustainer, the ultimate metaphysical cause, purpose and end of everything. The man is constantly in conflict within himself and with forces surrounding him. In Islam there is no segregation between religious and secular education. They are inseparable and indivisible. None of its aspects should be over-emphasized at the expense of the other.

"The ultimate aim of Islamic education lies in the inculcation of the concept of Allah in the minds and souls of God-fearing individuals and make them "good and righteous individuals who to lead happy and fruitful lives in this world and aspire, through good deeds, to achieve spiritual bliss in the hereafter""[(12)].

'It is inferred from the Qur'an that the aim of the prophets' missions is to establish justice, equity, and social equality and to demolish class barriers and walls[(13)].

According to al-Ghazzali's thinking on education, he favoured continuity and stability over change and innovation. 'The aim of education is to cultivate man so that he abides by the teachings of religion, and is hence assured of salvation and happiness in the eternal life hereafter'[(14)]. Children acquire personality, characteristics and behaviour through living in society and interacting with the environment. The family teaches them its language, customs and religious traditions etc. Therefore the main responsibility for children's education falls on the parents, who are partners in everything the children do, and this responsibility is subsequently shared by the teachers. Al-Ghazzali stresses the importance of childhood in character formation. A good upbringing will give children a good character and help them to live a righteous life; a bad upbringing will spoil their character and it will be difficult to bring them back to the straight path. It is therefore necessary to understand the special characteristics of this period in order to deal with the child in an effective and sound manner. Education is not limited to training the mind and filling it with information, but involves all aspects - intellectual, religious, moral and physical of the personality of the learner. It is not enough to impart theoretical learning; that learning must be put into practice. True learning is that which affects behaviour and whereby the learner make practical use of his knowledge.

For the establishment of a healthy human society, an intellectual, material, moral and spiritual environment is to be created in which a man is enable to develop his latent potentialities in harmony with the needs and aspirations of the society. The Islamic education aims that such an objective to ensure all the individuals acquire the qualities in agreement with the aforesaid state of affairs. Al-Ghazzali opines to have the main goal in their search for knowledge, the cultivation and perfection of the inner most self in this world, and proximity to God in the hereafter, rather than the attainment of high office or the acquisition of wealth or fame.

Curriculum Development

The setters of a curriculum should bear in mind some factors which are to be considered as the part and parcel of the prescribed course of study. When the theme of an Islamic curriculum is being planned, certain points are to be kept in the mind of the curriculum setters. A person who undergoes in the strains of Islamic curriculum should be prepared to live a life giving the actual place to the worldly and spiritual matters. The contents of the curriculum, the process of its transaction and evaluation etc. should also be in agreement with the nature of Islamic philosophy. However a man of integrated personality is expected to come out as a product on completion of a course of study under the Islamic curriculum.

Islamic Philosophy does not regard life as an end in itself but a bridge towards the life hereafter. A fundamental difference between modern education and Islamic Philosophy is its views on life. Modern secular education merely considers life in this world as its final goal, whereas an Islamic education regards life as only a means of achieving happiness in the hereafter. So, the Islamic curriculum should be framed with a view to realizing this goal.

The curriculum of any society will reflect its concepts of issues, the ideology and culture it inherits, the goals which it intends to achieve etc. Islamic curriculum familiarizes the individual with his relation to his fellow beings and other creatures, his responsibilities in life, duties and role in the society, his social relation and his relationship with the universe as a whole.

Islamic curriculum allows freedom of thought. It promotes the belief that the social order in Islam is based on unity, equality and fraternity. It brings up the individuals to respect each other. It aims to bring up an individual who is lenient, kind-hearted and has good manners and individual who neither maltreats nor does injustice to others, but forgives those who trespass against him.

The Islamic curriculum is based on unity of God, guidance of prophets, the concept of the day of resurrection and man living the life as a servant of God obeying His commandments. It develops tolerance, brotherhood, love, mercy and righteousness in the individuals so that a truly Islamic society may come into existence. It will develop the habit of consultation with each other in all matters "... and consult them in affairs (of moment); ..."(15) So the maximum benefit can be enjoyed by each individual and almost all the problems are to be solved among the individuals maintaining harmony and co-operation, without any conflict. Islamic curriculum develops in the individual, the feeling of shouldering responsibilities and performing his duties sincerely, in time. Such individual may not think on enjoying his rights before admitting the rights of other people from him.

"Al-Ghazzali distinguishes clearly between two types of curricula. (i) Obligatory knowledges which must be studied by everyone. It includes the religious sciences and related disciplines such as linguistics and literature; (ii) Optional knowledge, which are to be learned according to the interest and capacities of the pupil. They are in turn divided into: (a) revealed sciences and (b) non-revealed sciences"[(16)].

The criterion governing the choice of subjects is their usefulness for the student and for society. Hence religious subjects are preferred, since they are conducive to the Godliness of the eternal life hereafter. Al-Ghazzali divides each branch of knowledge into three levels: elementary, intermediate and advanced (Primary, Secondary and higher), and he lists the books that may be studied at each level of the various sciences and subjects of study. Adequate knowledge of Arabic should be prescribed to read it fluently with full comprehension. (2)Mathematics and physical sciences should be advanced enough to enable the students to pursue their studies later at science faculties. (1)The curriculum should include, in addition to religious subjects and Arabic, the study of history, geography and a foreign language etc.

"Ibn Khaldun distinguishes three types of knowledge corresponding to as many 'degrees of thought': practical knowledge, which allows us to act in the world in a controlled fashion; 'empirical intelligence - a knowledge of what we must or must not do and of what is good or evil and which guides us in our relations with our fellows; and lastly theoretical knowledge of everything that exists in the world, which we conquer by our 'speculative intelligence."[(17)] When a curriculum for

Islamic education is being framed, the views of Imam al-Ghazzali and Ibn-Khaldun are to be given proper place.

The bases of Islamic curriculum are mainly Qur'an and Sunnah. So, it is the prime duty of the curriculum setters not to include any element which may adversely affect the Qur'anic principles. However, a man of integrated personality is expected to come out as a product on completion of the Islamic curriculum

The Islamic curriculum is ideologically oriented; hence the nature and contents of it and the syllabi will be of the same nature. Islamic education is a life-long process. So, possibility of continuity should be ensured in all stages of education. Qur'anic concept of man is that he is, dignified honourable human being, "the vicegerent of God on earth"[(18)]. Accordingly, the curriculum should be framed including the relevant and appropriate topics for preparing the man to undergo a stream of education that will prepare him to perform effectively the duties entrusted upon him.

Curriculum Transaction

The Qur'anic methods of education are Zikr and Fikr (Remembrance and contemplation) and it is based on 'Tauhid' (Unity of God), 'Risalat' (Prophethood) and 'Akhirat' (Life Hereafter). Allah is the Creator, Cherisher, Master and Sovereign of the earth and the whole Universe. All human beings are His servants and therefore, are subject to

His Laws. Allah has sent His Messengers for the guidance of humanity. Muhammed is the last Messenger of Allah. All human beings are destined to die one day; stand the trail before their Lord to submit their accounts for their omissions and commissions in this world. The earth and all that in it belong to Allah; and man is His Vicegerent on earth. The curriculum should reflect these basic principles.

The Muslims used certain methodologies to transact the Islamic curricula. Islamic curricula adopt inimitable and indispensable methodologies mentioned in the Holy Qur'an. In the primary and intermediate stages, the Holy Qur'an is given a place of utmost importance. The memorization of certain amount of Qur'an is to be made compulsory requisite for every pupil. All branches of humanities should be free from any material that conflicts with Islamic faith at all stages of education. Questioning and answering was one of the methods of instruction next to memorization. Discussions and debates were conducted among learned people as the ways of instruction. Sermons consisted of examples or parables also were accepted in the education circles as the medium to transact knowledge. Many books were translated from Arabic into other languages. And some books from other languages also were translated into Arabic. Certain amount of knowledge was transformed to Arabic and to other languages by this steps. The methods of experimentation and observation were also adopted as a technique of acquiring knowledge.

Small group learning method was adopted by the Muslims. The learning material was distributed in small groups of pupils and they had acquired it in the level of mastery learning. Mastery learning, peer group learning and activity-oriented learning etc. are the learning techniques adopted by the Muslims in the early system of Islamic education.

The success of transacting the curriculum mainly depends on the initiative taken by the teacher in enthusiasing the child towards study for self-confidence, self-reliance and self-realization. The mission of Prophet was to teach the people God's message. Holy Qur'an says. "It is He Who sent amongst the unlettered an apostle from among themselves, to rehearse to them, His signs, to sanctify them and to instruct them in Scripture and Wisdom, although they had been, before, in manifest error."[(19)]

Islamic education culminates in the union of knowledge with action. The Islamist teacher should possess higher ideals and nobler pattern of behaviour always, especially in the presence of the child and thereby encourages him to imitate and act accordingly. This helps character formation in the child. The teacher should be an expert in his field. The learning items should be presented to the children with their active co-operation and participation with interest. The method of teaching, to a large extent, depends upon the capacity, competence and academic qualification of the teacher. He has to adopt the apt method, in teaching, which is relevant and well-fitted according to the level of children.

According to al-Ghazzali 'the value of learning lies in its usefulness and veracity' He says: "education is not merely a process whereby the teacher imparts knowledge which the pupil may or may not absorb, after which the teacher and pupil each go their separate ways; rather, it is an 'interaction' affecting and benefiting the teacher and pupil equally, the former gaining merit on giving instruction and the later cultivating himself through the acquisition of knowledge"[20].

While transacting the proposed curricula, the teacher has to listen to maintain the interest of the child. He may adopt the method from easy to difficult and known to unknown. 'The teachers should not push the pupils beyond their capacity, nor attempt to bring them to a level of knowledge which they cannot absorb'[21]. Al-Ghazzali proposes a "professional code of ethics for teachers, who should practise what they preach, and be an example to their pupils and to people in general"[22].

The teacher should take into account the differences in character and ability among pupils, and deal with each one of them appropriately. Among the principles governing the art of teaching, al-Ghazzali stresses that "teaching should be linked with concrete situations and it emphasizes the need for various types of knowledge and skills. Whenever a particular knowledge or skill is needed, it should be taught in such a way as to meet that need and be functional"[23]. He also stresses that learning is only effective when it is put into practice, and is aimed at inculcating the right habits rather than simply memorizing information. Al-Ghazzali comes close to the idea of 'proficiency learning' and he recommends that "the teacher should not move on from one subject matter to another without ensuring that the pupil has mastered the first subject and he advises that the teacher should pay attention to the interconnectedness of knowledge and the relation between its various branches"[24]. Also he advises the pupils to study each subject thoroughly before going on to another, bearing in mind the logical sequence and interconnections of the various disciplines. Finally, he counsels a gradual and patient approach in teaching"[25]. Al-Ghazzali stresses the importance of Activity based class room learning, Mastery-learning etc. which are considered as very effective teaching techniques in modern times. He is very close to the idea of the 'society of teachers and learners'. In his opinion, 'teaching is not the duty of scholars and teachers alone; anyone who learns something has a duty to teach it.'[26]

Teacher -Pupil Interaction

Education is the full realization of man's latent potentialities through proper nourishment, and evolutionary development of both body and mind. Therefore Islamic Philosophy of education always insists upon that a right use of intellectual energies can be attained by actual participation in the real life problems, an appreciation of the true perspective of things around us, that it is more blessed to give than to receive, in service to others, in service to humanity and finally in service to Allah and that a social conduct which is based on truth, honesty, charity, self control, resolution, courtesy and tolerance.

According to Islamic concept of education, learners should come into close contact with teachers and not rely mainly upon textbooks. Character building is the main objective of Qur'anic education. The Holy Qur'an states: "Verily you have in the Prophet of God an excellent model"(33:21). The duties and responsibilities entrusted to an educator are, in many respects, identical with the prophetic mission. It is the duty of the educators to provide their learners with the sure means of guidance. According to Al-Ghazzali, the teacher should be a model and an example, not merely a purveyor or medium of knowledge. His work is not limited to the teaching of a particular subject; rather, it should encompass all aspects of the personality and life of the pupil. The pupil, in turn, has a duty to consider the teacher as a father, to whom he owes obedience and respect.

Unlike any other professional, the duty of a teacher has no beginning or end. Actually he is a man of full-time day and night service. After one day's duty is over, he has to think of the next day's activities. He has to prefix the item and extent of work to be undertaken on the next day; prepare the tools and techniques for presenting the activity, think about the types of assistance for the presentation of activity etc. And he has to remake and re-wind his own knowledge and experience in the area (subject) for the successful transaction of the subject matter.

Al-Ghazzali insists that the students should safeguard the interest of their teachers, and practise the good lessons they give. It is obligatory on their part to give him respect with affection. This instruction is a very relevant message to the present day student community which has no identity of its own and is not bothered to mind any social values.

According to al-Ghazzali, all men ought to teach what they learned by any means, wheneverelse and from whereeverelse and thereby interact with the society. Al-Ghazzali recognizes the duties of a teacher as follows:

1. He will show kindness and sympathy to students and treat them as his own children. The duties of teacher are more than those of a parent. A father is the immediate cause of this transient life; but a teacher is the cause of immortal life. By teacher, I mean the teacher of the sciences of the hereafter, or the sciences with the objects of hereafter.

2. The second duty of teacher is to follow the usages and ways of the prophet. In other words he should not take remuneration for teaching, but nearness of God.

3. The third duty of a teacher is that he should not withhold from his students any advice. After he finishes the outward sciences he should teach them the inward sciences

4. The fourth duty of teacher is to dissuade his students from the evil ways with care, caution and sympathy.

5. The fifth duty of the teacher is that he should not belittle the value of other sciences before his students. The teacher of one learning should prepare his students for other learning.
6. The sixth duty of the teacher that he should do to teach his students upto the power of their understanding. God commanded not to give your property to fools.
7. The seventh duty of the teacher is that he should teach his backward students only such things as are clear and suited to their limited understanding.
8. Eighth duty of the teacher is that he should himself do what he teaches and should not give a lie to his teachings. Action of the teacher should not be contrary to what he teaches.

However, teaching and all the connecting activities should be by way of interaction with the entire society.

Educational Management

Effective management is an inevitable factor to achieve the proposed goal of any programme. Educational matter, especially of Islamic education, also do not exempt from the above condition. In the system of Islamic education, the pupils are governed by the spiritual and ethical values of Islam. They are trained not to satisfy for the material worldly benefit, but to develop as rational, righteous beings and bring about the spiritual, moral and physical welfare of their families, people and mankind. Islamic education is an education which shapes the sensibility of pupils in such a manner that their attitude of life, actions, decisions and approach to all kinds of knowledge are perfected. Traditional Muslim education acted in harmony with all other activities. The mosque was the heart of all religious activities and apex of the whole system. The community of Muslim is founded upon a creed and the constant values of a firm faith which gives its members their distinctive character and unmistakable Islamic personality.

The management on Islamic education mainly insisted upon the teacher not only to be a man of mere learning but also to be a person of virtue, a pious man whose conduct by itself could have an impact upon the minds of the youngsters; it was not only what he taught that mattered; but what he did; the way he conducted himself, his deportment in class and outside also were all expected to conform to an ideal which his pupils could unhesitatingly accept. Education must be for learning. Learning is an active process of change. In fact, to be alive is to be constantly active and changing. The world changes every moment not only socially, but also biologically as well as psychologically. The educator and the learner both have to make adaptations accordingly. The entrusted personnels for management have to ensure these things in time. Islamic education stresses the value of close co-operation between the school and the home in the up-bringing of the child. It should be listened to equal opportunities for all Muslims to seek and acquire knowledge and vocational and academic guidance of students according to their individual potentialities or inclinations and social needs. This can be done by well planning with foresightedness in educational management.

As the management of educational careers, direct instruction was adopted in the educational institutions. The prophet Muhammed's chief mission was to teach the humanity the message of God. He used to give lectures to impart the knowledge to the fellowmen. He emphasized the need to instruct children considering their individual differences, previous experiences, attitudes and aptitudes. He emphasized the influence of learning by action and by sensory training and also stressed the importance of mother tongue.

The Mosques

The Central Institution in the Islamic education was the mosque. From the days of Prophet and for quite a few centuries thereafter it was a place not only for saying prayers, but also for taking political decision, place for receiving deputation of persons who would visit Amiru'l Mu'minin on official matters. It was also a place for rendering judicial decisions to resolve conflicts between individuals. "The mosques were the centres of elementary and higher learning in the period of medieval Islam. Institutions for higher learning were also established either alongwith the mosques or under the control of it"[(27)].

The Madrasah system

The education in the early centuries of Islam was being carried out in 'madaris'. These type of schools were connected with a major mosque. The students were accommodated with boarding and lodging facilities. They were not restricted to finish their studies within a particular period of time as modern universities do. No specific degrees were conferred upon them. Most of the Islamic intellectual sciences today are performed outside formal institution. Very often a library was attached alongwith the madrasah.

According to Islam, education is a powerful instrument for bringing about social change and to put an end to ignorance and superstitions. A teacher is held in high esteem in the Islamic society, eventhough he may not be wealthy. Learning and scholarships have always been the most priced virtues in Islamic society, so imparting education has been considered a meritorious deed. "to be present in an assembly of a learned man is better than visiting one thousand sick men and attending one thousand funerals"[(28)]. Muslims have contributed their mite towards the establishment of Maktabs ad Madrasas and provided assistance to students in the form of stipend, books, food and the like.

No formal educational institutions were found during the early days of Islam. Classes were held in the compounds of mosques, in cells and dormitories attached to the residence of the 'Ulema'. The expenses of the madrasas were met from the revenue earned from large estate given as endowments. Certain madrasas had libraries and hospitals attached to it.

Many distinguished men of Islam used to teach his pupils many subjects at his home just like the 'Gurukula' system prevalent in India. The Mugal ruler, Aurangazeb, different in outlook and character, advocated many reforms in education which continued to engage the attention of scholars even today. The Imam of mosque imparted free instruction to pupils, in addition to his duty to lead daily prayers etc. This marked the beginning of free education among Muslims and still continue even today.

One of the objectives of the present study has been to understand the general features of Islamic Philosophy of Education in terms of its aims and objectives, curriculum development, curriculum transaction, teacher-pupil interaction and educational management. Above mentioned analysis of Islamic system of Education has revealed its characteristic features as far as the objective is concerned. It has been found that Islam has its own aims and objectives which can be found not only in the writings of Imam. al-Ghazzali and Ibn Khaldun etc. but in several contexts in Qur'an and Hadiths also. History of Islam has proved that Islamic Educational Institutions had their own curriculum and the philosophy of curriculum centred round the Islamic epistemology and axiology which were based on Qur'an and Hadith. As far as curriculum transaction is concerned Islamic education had from its very inception followed very scientific methods like observation, generalization, discussion, debates, sermons, memorization, lateral thinking, activity orientation, meaningful learning, pragmatic approach etc. It is evident from the above mentioned descriptions that Islamic Philosophy gave vital importance to maintaining relationship between pupils and teachers. It is evident that in the system of education there was constant and regular interaction between teachers and pupils which helped to mould the character of the pupils. It has been established that the educational activities were well planned. The educational institutions and activities connected with them were managed with the co-operation of the community. It is stated that the mosque was the central institution in the system of Islamic education and Madrasas were attached to it. The facilities for students' staying in the educational institutions were made which was later adopted by the system of modern education.

Based on these historical facts one can come to the conclusion that there was healthy teacher-pupil interaction which resulted in the increase in knowledge of the students and their character formation. Besides, the new system of arrangements made for the studies, and stay of the students make it clear that there was a system of management which was often supported by the rulers of the region as well as the community as a whole. The system of educational management was carried out in the interest of the society based on the principles of Islam.

Based on these facts the investigator has to state that the hypothesis formed by him that there exists a system of education evolved from the

Islamic Philosophy with specific characteristic, is correct. These characteristic features belong to: aims and objectives, curriculum development, curriculum transaction, teacher-pupil interaction and educational management.

3. Islamic Philosophy: Its Influence on Modern Education

Muslim philosophy influenced Western thought in several ways. It initiated the humanistic movement, introduced the historical science and scientific method, helped the Western scholastics in harmonizing philosophy with faith, laid the foundations of Italian Renaissance and moulded the modern European thought down to the time of Emmanuel Kant. The greatest boon that the Muslim East bestowed upon the West is the scientific or inductive method of inquiry. The influence of Muslim method of observation and experiments on the West has been recognized. It is believed that Rojer Bacon had introduced the experimental methods to the West. He was no more than one of the agents of Muslim science and methods to Christian Europe; and he never wearied of declaring that knowledge of Arabic and Arab science was for his contemporaries the only way to true knowledge. In the West, even upto the ninth /fifteenth century, philosophy and science were regarded as antagonistic to religion. Hence the teachings of Aristotelianism and Averroism were banned, Bruno was burnt, Kepler was persecuted and Galileo was forced to retract. Muslim thinkers had harmonized faith with reason.

Traces of the influence of Islamic philosophy can be identified in almost all the branches of modern knowledge and education. An examination of the origin of the influences that affected the modern knowledge, including in the field of education will naturally reveal the glory of the Arab scholars and their contributions to the humanity. There was a period in the European history known as 'Dark Ages' which is marked by an arrested growth of culture and civilization for a period of five to six centuries. But it was a 'golden age', for the Arabs in the 'Middle East' and the lands which they influenced. The influence of Islamic Philosophy in the areas of modern education, as already hypothesized can be examined with regard to: (i) Aims and Objectives (ii) Curriculum development (iii) Curriculum transaction (iv) Teacher-Pupil interaction and (v) Educational management.

A discussion and comparison of the educational philosophy of select philosophers of modern education who lived after the 'Renaissance' is attempted here with a view to examining whether there was any influence of the Islamic thinkers who lived before the period of 'Renaissance' on their thoughts. The possibility of influence of the views of earlier thinkers on the later ones can be legitimately assumed.

"From the point view of Western Civilization, relationship with the Muslim world have been of crucial importance since the early seventh century".[(29)] "When we consider all the contributions of the Byzantines and the Muslims to Western culture, we are altogether justified in saying that much light came from East".[30]

As recorded by Brinton "as time passed, some Westerners married Easteners, and a race of half breeds came to existence. Even those who did not intermarry often had their houses, palaces or churches built by native craftsmen. They wore oriental clothes, let their beards grow and ate squatting on carpets, hired Muslim physicians, joined Muslims in tournaments and hunts, shared certain shrines and debated the theology of each other's religions. These Easternised Westerners were suspected to pilgrims, freshly arrived from the West. Yet the visitors who went back to the West probably has a greater effect on European society than did those who stayed in the East"[31].

The contribution of Islamic philosophy was of equal importance to the West. Islamic philosophy became the primary vehicle for the transmission of Greek philosophy to the medieval Europe. The enormous accomplishments of Islamic philosophy and science were the product of men of genius, multitalented intellectuals who often mastered the major disciplines of medicine, mathematics, astronomy and philosophy. There were the 'renaissance' men of classical Islam. Comenius, Rousseau and John Dewey - all the three thinkers lived after the period of Renaissance. Hence it is probable that they might have been influenced by their predecessors, the Islamic thinkers. The famous historian Arnold Toynbee opined that in the Muqaddimah to his Universal history Ibn Khaldun has conceived and formulated as philosophy of history which is undoubtedly the greatest work of its kind that has ever yet been created by any mind in any time or place. In his chosen field of intellectual activity he appears to have been inspired by no predecessor. As regards the science or philosophy of history, Arabian literature was adorned by one most brilliant name. Neither the classical nor the medieval Christian world can show one of nearly the same brightness as Ibn Khaldun.... As a theorist in history he had no equal in any age or country... Plato, Aristotle, Augustine were not his peers and all others were unworthy of being even mentioned alongwith him... He was admirable alike by his originality and segacity, his profoundity and his comprehensiveness.

Aims and Objectives

Islamic philosophy insists on creation of 'good and righteous man' through education. Islamic education aims at the alround development of the personality of man to make him capable of discharing his duties to the Creator and his co-creations. The Muslim philosopher, al-Gazzali views "education as a process which forms the character of the individual and reforms the society.[(32)] Comenius, the father of modern education opined that "Education is not merely the training of the child at school or in the house, it is a process affecting man's whole life and the countless social adjustments he must make"[(33)]. According to him education is not limited to the actions of the school and family but is part and parcel of general social life. When the above remarks are juxtaposed, it can be seen that there is a thread of agreement in the educational ideas of al-Ghazzali and Comenius. So, naturally it can be felt that the hypothesis that Comenius, an educationist and a religious reformer, might have been influenced in his views, by the ideas of the Islamic philosophers like al-Ghazzali, who lived about five centuries before him as Ghazzali's works were very much used in the centres of learning in 17th and 18th centuries.

Ibn Rushd has his own views on education. He was a rationalist. He actually sought to harmonize the Qur'an and revelation with philosophy and logic. So, he has his own views on aims and objectives of education. He agreed with the eternity of the world as per the Aristotelian belief. According to Ibn Rushd, human intelligence is immaterial, immortal, abstract and separate from the individual. So, an individual must be given the education to realize this status of him. His views were the intellectual bases for the medieval Christianity. He recommended to maintain the continuity in study for acquiring knowledge, practically by reading sixteen hours a day even when he was seventy.

Ibn Rushd uses rationality to pursue knowledge of all kinds. Any suppression of the mind would violate this order. So, the objective of education, according to him, is to liberating of the mind by gradual progress. In the Christian and Jewish worlds, Ibn Rushd is renowned for his important hand in paving the way for the European Renaissance. His 'Great Commentary' made a deep impression on Western students and caused an absolute upheaval in the West.

According to Ibn Khaldun, by education one should develop his reasoning power, he has to widen his power of thought. The theory of gradation was presented by Ibn Khaldun and it has been widely accepted by the modern education system. He recommended keen observation and deep thinking for learning. He suggested the objective of early education as developing the power of expression by giving emphasis on language. The famous historian Arnold Toyenbee was influenced by the views of Ibn Khaldun on history and thereby the influence on modern education.

John Dewey, developed a theory of knowledge that contested the dualism of the mind and world, thought and action, which had marked the Western philosophy since the seventeenth century; he views "the manifestations of an Absolute Mind for instrumental functions that has evolved in order to serve the interests of human survival and welfare" (34). The Key note of his educational philosophy is 'pragmatism'.

By giving vocationalised training through the laboratory schools, John Dewey advocated the message of dignity of labour. Through all these recommendations John Dewey, the twentieth century educationist agrees with the expositions of Islamic Philosophy which stands for the unity of mankind and recommends an admissible vocation for one's livelihood. The saying of the Phrophet of Islam was that knowledge is to be practised. Hence Islam has advised every human being to engage himself in the vocations to ensure the livelihood for his family members, and for himself and for his fellow-beings who deserve to expect from him, as well. Dewey's statement 'to serve the interests of human survival and welfare' is fully in agreement with what Prophet instructed some fourteen centuries before.

Rousseau remarks in his important book "Emile" : "A man who wished to regard himself as an isolated being, attached to absolutely nothing and quite self sufficient, could not help but be wretched"[(35)]. According to him, "schools are to be made agencies of social reform rather than agencies of social reproduction".[(36)] Through these remarks, Rousseau also reminds that education should make individual to work for the wellbeing of the society which is in agreement with the Islamic Philosophy.

Rousseau advocated in his influential essay on political ethics 'social contract' the necessity of 'return to nature'. By this view he admits the Qur'anic view on the importance of maintaining balance of the nature. Qur'an indicates that: 'Land and sea is affected by turmoil by the misdeeds of men'.

Curriculum development

As seen in the earlier part, Islamic philosophy does not view the life as an end but a means to the endless life, hereafter. But modern philosophies of education consider life in this world as its final goal. Eventhough the views on educational philosophy varies, there may be some similarities in developing the curricula based on each philosophical outlook and its transactional strategies.

The curriculum based on Islamic philosophy must be fit to acquaint the learners with his relations to the Creator and the other creatures around him, his responsibilities, duties and role in the society, his mode of approach to all others etc. All the Islamic philosophers kept these things in mind when they developed their philosophical ideas and curricula and determined its transactional methodology.

Al-Ghazzali recommended a life-oriented curriculum, which must have provision to estimate the ability of the students. He advocated the primary education for women and recommended home science for them. He insisted to include physical science for children. He stated, "philosophy is nothing more than commonsense and regulated thinking, so it cannot give us truth equal to revelation"(37).

Ibn-khaldun made a most notable suggestion that the early education is to develop the power of expression by study of language; language learning is nothing but a matter of habit formation.(38) His ideas held wide currency in Europe in those days. Probably, Ibn-khaldun's ideas might have influenced Comenius who also directed to teach language at first in primary classes. He advocated everything in the curriculum that might be pleasurable to the children.

Ibn Rushd is famous in Europe for his theory of the 'Unity of the Intellect'. He also presented 'two truths theory'; one truth for philosophers, which is philosophy and the other is for masses, it is religion. He tried to harmonize the Qur'an and revelation with philosophy and logic. Ibn Rushd recommended to developing the curriculum comprised his main ideas which influenced the modern education. His main ideas are : allegorical interpretation of the scriptures, the theory of two truths, Pan-psychism, eternity and potentiality of matter and emancipation of women etc. He viewed that man must be free from all oppressions and injustice. The curriculum must be suited to realize this goal. Considering all his contributions, it can be undoubtedly stated that no other Muslim thinker influenced the West than Ibn Rushd.

According to Rousseau, education is the first and foremost matter of intelligence, able to grasp the laws that govern the development of human nature. He made the child the focus of the educational process. He opposed the idea that the image of the child was the fruit of the sin. Scholars have endeavored to sort out Rousseau's borrowings both from precursors and from brilliant contemporaries.(39) Here Rousseau agrees with the Islamic teaching that 'all the children are born innocent'.[40] His thinking, systematic in its form, aimed constantly for unity. He might have been influenced by the Islamic idea of the 'unity of man.'

John Dewey opines, "the critical task of education is to help children to develop character, the habits and virtues- that would enable them to achieve self realization.[41]

Curriculum Transaction

The Qur'anic method of instruction is 'Zikr and Fikr' (Remembrance and Contemplation). By undergoing a prescribed course of study under a planned curriculum in the Islamic philosophy, a pupil should develop an awareness that he is destined to die one day without any prior knowledge of it and stand the trial before the Al-mighty Allah being accountable to Him for all his thoughts, words and actions in the world. Qura'n says, " every soul shall have a taste of death: And only on the Day of judgement shall you be paid your full recompense..... For the life of the world is but goods and chattels of deception"[42].

Comenius advocated 'nature's way'; ie. he recommended learning about things through sensory experience. He introduced the system of 'Pansophy', ('Pansophia': universal knowledge) which has an Islamic touch in its call to universal wisdom and thereby unity of mankind. He recognized international education to realize the aim of achieving the oneness of humanity for which Islam strongly instructed. He was of the idea of founding of universal schools. "a metaphysician, no idea of requirements of the experimental, psychological or even educational research, substituted the discussion of ideas for the analysis of facts' [43]. Comenius may undoubtedly be considered "as one of the precursors of the genetic idea in developmental psychology, and as the founder of a system of progressive instruction adjusted to the stage of development the pupil has reached"[44]. Comenius says in his 'Great Didactic', though this schools be different, we donot wish to teach them different things, but rather the same things in a different manner. I mean, all things which can make men truly men, and the learned truly learned; they should be taught in consideration of the pupils' age and the standard of his prior preparation, which should always tend gradually upward"[45].

In the chapter of 'Principles of Facilitating Teaching and Study', the 'Great Didactic' remarks three rules: (i) The class instruction be curtailed as much as possible, namely to four hours, and the same length of time be left for private study. (ii) The pupil be forced to memorize as little as possible that is to say only the most important things; of the rest they need only grasp the general ideas. (iii) Everything be arranged to suit the capacity of the pupil, which increases naturally with study and age.[46] Ibn Masu'd reported: Prophet used to take care of us in preaching by selecting a suitable time, so that we might not get bored. (He abstained from pestering us with sermons and knowledge all the time). Comenius admits Ghazzali that 'the teacher must show that his actions are based on paternal affection and are destined to build up the character of his pupils'.

"Do not undertake any teaching without first arousing the interest of the pupil; always offer something which will be both agreeable and useful to the pupils' minds will come forward eagerly, with everyday attention.[(47)] Here Comenius' ideas go alongwith the advice of Prophet Muhammed that any teaching may be imparted after arousing the interest of the pupils and at the apt time, etc.

Imam Ghazzali gave importance to the method of observation and experimentation. He agreed that all philosophical assumptions, speculations and hypotheses should be judged and verified with reference to facts, for otherwise, they would be empty and meaningless. The pupil has to acquire the ability to distinguish between good and evil. The teacher should be a model and ought to be imitated by the pupils in all the actions and thereby his character will be formulated and can abstain from evil. He suggested to teach the subjects in their order of utility and importance. He advocated for life-oriented and activity-oriented education, which John Dewey, the eminent educationist approved as the most effective method of curriculum transaction. Al-Ghazzali presented so many things to be adopted in the class-room teaching. Consideration to previous knowledge, teaching from easy to difficult, the use of learning aids to make the class more alive and effective etc. were the strategies in the class-room teaching-learning process and were strongly recommended in the modern system of education. By these, it is unquestionable that the methods of class-room teaching propounded by al-Ghazzali, have immensely influenced the modern system of education.

According to Ibn Rushd 'it is evident that God had created in us faculties by means of which we can acquire things which are opposed by nature' which proves that freedom of choice exists. He does not agree with the immortality of the individual intellect. Being an advocate of intellectual liberty, he opposed the rigid minds of scholars. The transactional methodology of curriculum should be in agreement with his liberal views. Known as 'Averroes' in the West, he played a leading role in the revival and development of Christian scholasticism. His works originated heated dialogue among the scholars in Christian Europe and influenced the West for four centuries from the twelfth to the sixteenth. Ibn Rushd made the greatest impact on Europe in philosophy.

Ibn-khaldun "recommends moderate use of authority and punishment, taking into consideration the personality of the pupil and the need to instruct without afflicting the pupil and killing his spirit"[(48)]. The students' receptivity and power of assimilation are to be taken in to account. He recommends three progressive stages in teaching: the first preparatory stage; second stage for deeper discussion and the third stage is of consolidation and mastery. He recommends the teacher to present the teaching material suited to the pupils' capacities, not to pass on to further details of the subjects before completely assimilating the first, not to teach two subjects together, dwell on a subject over too long a period, lest pupils should lose the interest. 'He emphasizes the method of discussion between the teacher and taught. He promoted the theory of gradation which is being adopted in modern education. He recommended forty minutes periods for school children, because the teacher cannot hold the attention of the pupils more than limited time[(49)]. Going through Comenius' ideas of education, and his instruction to teachers it can be found that they echo many of Ibn-Khalduns' ideas. Rousseau (like Dewey) advocates, 'activity method' aiming at making the child a technician in charge of its own knowledge[(50)].

John Dewey preferred to mode of inquiry and scientific investigation. He viewed thought and learning as a process of inquiry. He advocated to close the gap between thought and action and that learning must be related to current problems. His ideas are much closer to the teaching of the Prophet that 'the best of the knowledge is knowledge on contemporary issues"[(51)]. Qura'n says, "surely in the creation of the heavens and earth and in the alternation of night and day there are signs for men of understanding" [(52)]. What Qur'an advocates in this verse is that those who ponder about and go deeper in to the wonder of Creation can understand the realities of the universe.

Rousseau also wished to sustain the original personality of each pupil in the class rooms. "He sees that the child did not have to become anything other than what he was destined to be... living is the business that I wish to teach him; I grant, he will be, primarily, a man"[53]. Here Rousseau expresses his faith in destination and it relates to God and naturally reaches to Islamic Philosophical views on education.

Teacher- Pupil Interaction

Character building is the main objective of the education based on the Islamic Philosophy. As in all other matters, a believer has to rely on Allah's Prophet for the character formation also. Qur'an says : 'Verily you have in the Prophet of God, Muhammed an excellent exemplar[54]. For reforming the pupils' behaviour to an excellent exemplar, teacher is bound to behave always in an ideal manner.

In this regard Comenius commends that skillful and sympathetic treatment is necessary to instil love of learning into the minds of pupils; forceful application is not recommended at any stage. He is also against corporal punishment; plants grow and animals reproduce according to the season; education must also be imparted likewise in the apt situations. All these things will be shaped according to the approach of the teacher.

Rousseau says in Emile: 'A man who wished to regard himself as an isolated being, attached to absolutely nothing and quite self-sufficient, could not help but be wretched'[55]. A teacher is not expected to be like this.

A teacher in such a condition cannot interact with his pupils as a model. According to him, 'one is educating the heart, the head and the hand'. He held the view of that type of education proposed should be 'fitting to man' and well suited to the human heart[56]. As the child is the focus of the educational process, all the faculties of the child must be taken into account ie, the cognitive, affective and psychomotor domains of the child should be developed. Then only the education proposed should be 'fitting to man' and thereby the teacher and pupil can maintain a desirable style of interaction.

John Dewey views education as the process of ever increasing growth. Islam insists its followers to undergo education from the 'cradle to grave' ie: education is a life-long process aiming to develop the pupils' individuality. Here, Rousseau and John Dewey, both come nearer to the Islamic philosophy.

According to Al-Ghazzali, the objective of the education is utility which includes the material and spiritual aspects. The objective of education is formation, construction and completion of manners to distinguish between good and bad and abstain from evil. Here Rousseau and John Dewey give a place to developing the individuality of the pupil, as al-Ghazzali's thought.

Ibn Khaldun gave immense importance to maintaining the teacher-pupil relationship. Pupils are to be dealt with parental affection. Each pupil must be studied well, by the teacher. He should identify his abilities, shortcomings, socio-economic factors, habits and interests etc.

He should ensure to maintain the attention and interest of pupils in the class. For this, Ibn Khaldun recommended the duration of a class period as forty minutes. And he put forward the theory of gradation, which has been widely accepted in modern times. For all these purpose the teacher should understand each student well on interacting with each of them.

Educational Management

The management of any matter or programme should be suitable to realize the pre-planned goals of the same. Since the early days of Islam, it has been noticed to do and arrange the needful for implementing the educational activities. Mosque was the centre of education and culture and all other matters of the society were formed and performed under the control of the mosque. Maktabs and Madaris were founded later for imparting education. Then libraries and centres for translation of valuable books, were established in various parts of the Islamic world. It had been approved as the right centres of education to everybody. As a result, education could be imparted to all of its seekers.

Comenius and most of the educationists were in agreement with the Islamic view of equality and internationalism. Comenius claimed for 'the Universal right to education on a basis of equality, the system of education proposed is Universal by its very nature' and is intended for all men, irrespective of social or economic position, religion, race or nationality. He proposed "schemes for universal peace, plans for international societies for research, international organization for public education and a kind of international ministry of education"[57].

John Dewey also views democracy as a mode of association which provides the members of a society. By democracy, Rousseau ensures opportunity to everybody and thereby to establish equality and internationalism in every field of education and all walks of life as Islamic philosophy promotes.

Based on the above analysis, it can be legitimately concluded that the expansion of knowledge in the Muslim world had influenced the West in several ways since the Renaissance. Traces of evidences of this influence were indicated in the foregoing discussions. The influence of Islamic Philosophy on the Western system of education can therefore be found in the aims and objectives, curriculum development, curriculum transaction, teacher-pupil interaction and educational management to a certain extent, especially when the educational ideas of Comenius, Rousseau and John Dewey are examined. Therefore it can be stated that hypothesis No. III formed for the present study has been established to a large extent as Islamic Philosophy has directly or indirectly influenced in the theory and practice of education.

Throughout the analysis, a comparison of the select Islamic Philosophers of education represented by Imam Ghazzali, Ibn Rushd and Ibn Khaldun and modern philosophers of education represented by

Comenius, Rousseau and John Dewey has been made as a part of examining the influence of Islamic Philosophy on modern education. This comparison has revealed that the idea of the Islamic Philosophers who lived in Arab countries before the Renaissance, had influenced the modern philosophers, especially Comenius, the father of modern education and Russeau, the great proponent of freedom in education. The very cardinal idea of Islamic philosophy that whatever is theorised or preached should be translated into practice has been reflected in John Dewey's ideas on education. Besides, Islamic scholars of the Medieval period and before that like Ibn Sina, Ibn Rushd, had shaped the scientific method of observation and experimentation which John Dewey has strongly advocated in his theories. Though there are no evidences to prove that John Dewey has borrowed this ideas from the Islamic philosophers, there are evidences to believe that he had received the ideas from the Renaissance writers and philosophers who had followed the Arab scholars. Therefore it can be stated that John Dewey was to a certain extend indirectly influenced by the Muslim scholars.

4. Influence of Islamic Knowledge on the West

It is recognized by all the educational thinkers that education is for the development of the alround development of the individual. An individual has to acquire the maximum informations in all the branches of education. So, an attempt has been made to list out the nature of influence that Islamic thinkers have made in different areas of knowledge which comprise the totality of education.

The Qur'an has given a great deal of emphasis on the need for observation of physical phenomena and natural processes and reflecting on whatever is observed. Man has been commanded to observe whatever is (visible) in the heavens and the earth. In order to discover a fact reflecting over whatever has been observed is essential. Those who do not use their senses for observation, and their minds for reflection have been compared to cattle; and they have been described even more astrayed than them[(58)]. Being inspired by these Qur'anic injunctions, "From the early days of Islam, the Muslims of all countries in general, and those of Arabia in particular, travelled extensively through plains and hills, rivers and oceans, forests and deserts in connection with Jihad, Hajj, trade etc. In the course of their travels they collected information on social, political, historical, geographical, economical, agricultural and other conditions of the lands they came across. As a consequence of the collection of such information, sciences such as history and geography were developed[(59)].

Aristotle's descriptions of physics etc. was not supported by even a single experiment. But the Muslim thinkers substantiated all of their statements by experiments and other evidences. Most of the Muslim rulers and officials were scholars in many subjects and hence the promotion of learning was seen throughout the Muslim world. They encouraged scholars from every part of the world, irrespective of their religion, race and nationality[60]. So throughout the reign of Muslim rulers in the Middle East, thinkers of other culture from various parts of the world, especially from the West, have either come and acquired the knowledge from the Muslims or benefited by increasing their knowledge by making use of books and other sources. From these things, there can be seen the influence of Islamic thought in many areas of knowledge extented by the Western thinkers. It can be ascertained without any hesitation that the revival of knowledge and Western culture has been made deriving inspiration from Islamic thought.

"Science is the most momentous contribution of Arab civilization to the modern world... It was not science only which brought Europe back to life. Other and manifold influences from the civilization of Islam communicated its first glow to European life[61]". Owing to the Islamic and Muslim scientific influences the volcano of knowledge had burst in Europe. Its thinkers and scientists had broken the chains of intellectual slavery. They boldly refuted the ecclesiastical theories, which were based on preposterous evidence, and proclaimed the results of their own investigations.

"The Muslims were of significance to the development of higher learning during the middle ages; they were outside the Christian society that dominated Europe. Not only did they promote education within their society, but they also served as translators and as intermediaries who brought ancient Greek thought and science to the attention of the European scholars"[(62)].

"Islam has consequently played a crucial role in world history, both as an important civilization in its own right, and as an intermediary between the civilizations of antiquity and those of the early modern world. This twofold aspect of the contribution of Islam is reflected in the history of science"[(63)].

Colin A. Ronan again says that "from what has been said here, there can be no doubt that the philosophers and scientists, geographers, natural historians and medical men of Arabian culture contributed materially to the sum of man's knowledge about the natural world"[(64)].

It is stated in the Encyclopaedia that "Islamic culture is the most relevant to European science. There was active culture contact between Arabic-speaking lands and Latin Europe at crucial periods. Ironically, the great age of Islam coincided with the low point of culture in Western Europe"[(65)].

It is generally recognized that the foundation of modern science on the basis of observation, experimentation and systematization, was laid by the Muslim savants. They started the work in the 8th century and assimilated whatever was achieved by their predecessors. They not only preserved and disseminated it by translating into Arabic, but, within a short period of time, systematized the knowledge acquired previously and began making significant advances of such fundamental nature that the phenomenal development of the modern era could not have been possible without the contributions made by them.

A number of academies were established throughout the Muslim world to carry out translations to grasp the foreign scientific works. The first academy of its kind, which contained a library and observatory also, named Baut-al-Hikmah (House of Wisdom) was set up by the Caliph al-Ma'mun. The Muslim scientists didn't believe in authoritarianism in science. They accepted the scientific conclusions of other subjects to their experimental verifications, and also made new observations and experiments leading to new discoveries. The following quotation from al-Biruni's 'Kitab al-Tafhim' throws light on the point: "And I have truly done what everyone is bound to do in respect of any particular science, that is, to accept gratefully the original contributions of his predecessors, to correct fearlessly the errors that come to his notice, and to preserve that what he himself discovers, and to leave it as a record for the future generations that are to follow him in time"[(66)].

In the various branches of science also, the contributions of Islamic thought are boundless. The Muslim scientists made the practical use of their scientific discoveries in technology also by observing the stars, preparing star maps for navigational purposes etc. "Ibn-Yunus made use of pendulum for the measurement of time, Ibn-Sina used air thermometer to find out air temperature. "Some of the other most important examples of scientific and technological developments of Muslim scientists are paper, compas, gun, gunpowder, inorganic acids and alkali etc., which brought about an unprecedented revolution in the human civilization" [(67)].

Some scientific works of Muslim experts like Kitab al-Qanun by Ibn Sina, Kitab al-Manazir by Ibn al-Haitham, Kitab al-Tasrif by al-Zahrawi, Kitab al-Ibar and al-Muqqaddimah by Ibn Khaldun and Kulliyat fi al-Tib by Ibn Rushd etc. were thoroughly studied in the Western academic institutions which exerted a great influence on scientific development in Europe. Kitab al-Qanun, a comprehensive medical work and is called 'canon' in the West. It was translated into Hebrew, Latin etc. and formed half the medical curriculum of the European universities in the later part of 15th century and about thirty editions of this work were published in Europe. From this it can be ensured the acceptance and influence of this single Muslim contribution that made in the Western world. George Sarton admits that the book of Ibn-al-Haitham, "Kitab al-Manazir (book of optics) exerted a great influence on European scientists for about 600 years"[(68)].

In the area of mathematics also the Islamic scholars recorded their landmark. The West learned the use of numerals from the Arabs, and therefore, called them the Arabic numerals. It was only in the 12th century that after learning from the Muslims the Western scholars were able to produce some literature on the numeral system, without columns, and completed by zero[(69)].

'The Muslims founded analytical geometry as well as plane and spherical trignometry. In the early stage of its development spherical trignometry was considered to be a part of astronomy which was made a separate branch of mathematics in the 13th century when it became sufficiently advanced"[70].

The zero was used by the Muslim mathematicians centuries before it was known in the West. The latin word 'ciphra' for zero is of Arabic origin; the Arabic word for it being 'sifr' meaning 'empty' or 'nil' to the book as a commentary on Ptolemy's Centiloquium, written as an ode by Ahmad Ibn Yusuf, influenced the medieval thought and through it Western mathematicians became aware of the theorem of Menelaos (about the triangle cut by a transversal). Sarton remarks: "A little stream of mathematical thought may be detected in the Latin writings, a stream which will gradually increase, but will not become truly significant until the 13th century when a sufficient amount of Arabic water will have flowed into it. Let us pass on to Islam. It is almost like passing from the shade to the open sun and from a sleepy world into one tremendously active"[71].

In the field of medicine and all its branches the medieval Muslims made unmatchable and invaluable contributions. The Muslims made researches in various branches of medical science. Until the 17th century these writtings were included in the syllabi of the European Universities. In France the Arabian Medicine was studied from 1410 to 1789. The medical curriculum was still largely based on Ibn Sina's 'Qanun' and on the ninth book of al-Razi's 'al-Mansuri'. The introduction of this science into Europe is an interesting chapter of history. According to Dr. Briffault, the Allopathic system of medicine is the outcome of Arabian Medicine[(72)].

The contributions of Muslims in the field of bacteriology are quite revolutionary. According to Browne, Muslims were fully aware of the theory of germs. Ibn Sina was the first to state that bodily secretion is contaminated by foul foreign earthly bodies before getting the infection. The Muslim physicians were the first to use the stomach tube for the performance of gastric lavage in the case of gas poisoning. They were fully aware of the principles of opotherapy centuries before Browne Sequard to whom this method of treatment is ascribed.

A book titled 'Al-Athar al Baqiyyah' in the University of Edinburgh contains an illustration showing an Arab physician performing Caesarian operation. Arabian pharmacology survived in Europe until the beginning of the 19th century[(73)].

In the areas of Geography and Astronomy also, the Muslim dignitories of the Middle ages, ensured their memorable presence. From seventh to the thirteenth century it was further developed by the Muslims and later on by Europeans. In the 14th and 15th centuries, the astrologers had great influence on the kings of the European countries[(74)]. A text on geography has not been written till 18th century, like that one written by the famous Arabian traveller and scholar, Al-Biruni wrote on India[(75)].

The Arabs gave importance to the experimental method which remained the basis of the method of 'Learning by Doing', the most recognized way of curriculum transaction now-a-days. The experimental method of Arabs was by Bacon's time widespread and eagerly cultivated throughout Europe[(76)]. No period shows more clearly than the enormous superiority of the Islamic culture, system of knowledge and people over the Christian world as the tenth century, when Islam was at the summit and Europe had come to a helpless stand still[(77)].

"Indeed, from recorded history, we are clear about the crucial role, which Islamic State played in scientific explorations during the Dark Ages of Europe' to complement the Qur'anic indications and in response to the encouragement from Islam"[(78)].

"Science arose in Europe as a result of new spirit of inquiry, of new methods of investigation, of the method of experiment, observation, measurement, of the development of mathematics in a form unknown to the Greeks, and that spirit and those methods were introduced into the European world by the Arabs"[(79)].

It can be concluded that Islamic thought played a vital role by influencing all the areas of Western scientific thought which naturally influenced the content and process of Western education.

REFERENCES

1. Ilyas, Dr. Muhammad, *Reaching the Revealed Truth through Science (Article, MWL Journal).*
2. Holy Qur'an, 112:1-2.
3. Ibid, 02:30.
4. Ibid, 49:13.
5. Al-Hadith
6. Holy Qur'an, 29:43.
7. Ibid, 02:197.
8. Ibid, 03:103.
9. Ibid, 03:110.
10. Ibid, 02:143.
11. Ibid, 03:104.
12. Afendi, al-Mohammed, *Curriculum and Teacher Education*: p.3.
13. Mutahhari, Ayathullah Murtaza, *Social and Historical Change An Islamic Perspective*: p.99.
14. Morsy, Zaghloul, *Thinkers on Education*. Vol. IV: p.524.
15. Holy Qur'an, 03:159.
16. Morsy, Zaghloul, *Thinkers on Education*. Vol. II: p.529.
17. Ibid, p.13.
18. *Al-Qur'an*, 02:30.
19. Ibid, 62:02
20. Morsy, Zaghloul, *Thinkers on Education*. Vol. II: p.530.

21. Ibid, p.526.

22. Ibid, p.532.

23. Morsy, Zaghloul, *Thinkers on Education*. Vol. IV: p.524.

24. Ibid, p.526.

25. Ibid, p.530.

26. Ibid, p.531.

27. Khan, Mohammed Sharif, *Islamic Education*. p.69.

28. Al-Hadith.

29. Brinton, *Civilization in the West*. p.173.

30. Ibid, p.179.

31. Ibid, p.187.

32. Karim, Maulana Fazlul, *Imam Ghazzali's Ihya Ulum-id-din*. Vol. I: p.134.

33. Morsy, Zaghloul, *Thinkers on Education*. Vol. I: p.175.

34. Ibid, p. 279.

35. Ibid, Vol. IV, p.432

36. Ibid, Vol. I, p. 283.

37. Khan, Mohammed Sharif, *Muslim Philosophy and Philosophers*. p.67.

38. Morsy, Zaghloul, *Thinkers on Education*. Vol. I: p.67.

39. Ibid, Vol. IV: p.424.

40. Al-Hadith.

41. Morsy, Zaghloul, *Thinkers on Education*. Vol. I: p.281.

42. Holy Qur'an, 03:185.

43. Morsy, Zaghloun, *Thinkers on Education*. Vol. I: p.173.

44. Ibid, p.177.
45. Ibid, p.178.
46. Ibid, p.178.
47. Ibid, p.179.
48. Ibid, Vol. III: p.14.
49. Ibid, p.15.
50. Ibid, Vol. IV: p.433.
51. Al – Hadith.
52. Holy Qur'an, 03:190.
53. Morsy, Zaghloul, *Thinkers on Education*. Vol. IV: p.425.
54. Holy Qur'an, 33:21.
55. Morsy, Zaghloul, *Thinkers on Education*. Vol. IV: p.432.
56. Ibid, p.435.
57. Ibid, Vol. I: p.182.
58. Holy Qur'an, 13:04.
59. Saud, Mohammed, *Islam and Evolution of Science*. p.42.
60. Browne, G, *Arabian Medicine*, p.76.
61. Briffault, Robert, The *Making of Humanity*. p. 202.
62. New Encyclopaedia. Vol. 8: p.323.
63. The Cambridge History of World Science. p.201.
64. Ibid, p.239.
65. The New Encyclopaedia Britannica. Vol. 16: p.368.
66. Al-Biruni, *Iran Society*. p.1.

67. Browne, G, *Arabic Medicine*. p.87.

68. Ibid, p.114.

69. Guillaume and Arnold, The Legacy of Islam. p. 386.

70. Sarton, George, *Introduction to the History of Science*. p.695.

71. Saud, Mohammad, *Islam and Evolution of Science*. p.26.

72. Browne, G, *Arabian Medicine*. p.71.

73. Ibid, p.724.

74. Browne, G, *Arabian Medicine*, p. 72.

75. Bernal, J.D., *Science in History* (Mal.) p.339.

76. Mirza, Dr. M.R. *Muslim Contribution to Science*, p. 117.

77. Ibid, p. 255.

78. Ilyas, Dr. Muhammad, *Preaching the Revealed Truth through Science*. Article MWL Journal p. 34.

79. Briffault, Robert, *The Making of Humanity*. p.191

CONCLUSION AND SUGGESTIONS

CHAPTER VI

CONCLUSION AND SUGGESTIONS

- The study in retrospect
- Hypotheses of the study
- The objectives of the study
- The Hypotheses
- Methodology of the study
- Important Findings
- Suggestions for further study

CONCLUSION AND SUGGESTIONS

The Study in Retrospect

The present study was aimed to identify the general and characteristic features of Islamic philosophy and its views on education and to trace its influence if any, on the Western education. It was carried out mainly on comparing the thoughts of Islamic philosophers such as Imam Ghazzali, Ibn Rushd and Ibn Khaldun etc. with the educational thoughts of modern thinkers like Comenius, Rousseau and John Dewey etc.

The objectives of the study were:

- To estimate the main characteristic features of Islamic philosophy.
- To list out the general features of Islamic philosophy in terms of: Aims and Objectives, Curriculum Development, Curriculum Transaction, Teacher-pupil Interaction and Educational Management etc.
- To assess the nature of the Influence of Islamic philosophy on the modern education in terms of Aims and Objectives, Curriculum Development, Curriculum Transaction, Teacher-pupil Interaction and Educational Management etc.
- To examine the educational philosophies of both Islamic and Western philosophers such as Imam-Ghazzali, Ibn Khaldun and Comenius, Rousseau, John Dewey from the comparative philosophical point of view.

- To locate the process of learning followed in the Islamic Educational Institutions.
- To understand the influence of Islamic knowledge on the West.

Hypotheses of the Study

The hypotheses formulated have been verified with reference to available original sources: i.e. primary sources and secondary sources and their tenability has been verified.

The study has been carried out on the basis of the major hypotheses:

i. Islam has an independent philosophy which can be interpreted in terms of (a) nature of man and his place in the world (b) nature of knowledge and (c) nature of values.

ii. There exists a system of education evolved from Islamic philosophy and it can be identified and described in terms of its characteristics related to:

   a) Aims and Objectives
   b) Curriculum development
   c) Curriculum transaction
   d) Teacher-pupil interaction
   e) Educational management

iii. Islamic philosophy has directly or indirectly influenced the theory and practice of modern education and this influence can be identified and described in terms of its features related to:

a) Aims and Objectives

b) Curriculum development

c) Curriculum transaction

d) Teacher-pupil interaction

e) Education management

iv. It is possible to identify the direct or indirect influence of Islamic philosophy on modern theories and practice of education by comparing the select representative philosophers like Imam Ghazzali, Ibn Khaldun and Ibn Rushd with Comenius, Rousseau and John Dewey.

Methodology of the Study

The objectives of the study enabled the investigator to conduct the study employing a combination of historical and analytical methods based on intensive study of primary and secondary sources.

Tenability of the Hypotheses

The analysis throws light on the tenability of the hypotheses set for the study.

The first hypothesis formed for the study that Islam has an independent philosophy which can be interpreted in terms of nature of man and his place in the world, nature of knowledge and nature of values has been undoubtedly established.

The second hypothesis that there exists a system of education evolved from Islamic philosophy in terms of its characteristics related to: aims and objectives, curriculum development, curriculum transaction, teacher-pupil interaction and educational management, has been found correct.

The third hypothesis that the Islamic philosophy has directly or indirectly influenced the theory and practice of modern education and it can be identified and described in terms of: aims and objectives, curriculum development, curriculum transaction, teacher-pupil interaction and educational management, has been substantiated to a large extent.

As hypothesized for the study it has been possible to identify the direct or indirect influence of Islamic philosophy on modern theories and practice of education by comparing the select representative philosophers like Imam Ghazzali, Ibn Khaldun and Ibn Rushd with Comenius, Rousseau and John Dewey, has also been found correct. .

Important Findings

From the analysis it has been found that:

- The philosophy of modern education has been considerably influenced by the Islamic philosophy.

- The philosophy of Islam is a unique one which is rather different from other schools of philosophies of the West.
- Islamic philosophy has a firm epistemology and axiology which are based on divine revelation of knowledge.
- It has independent views on the nature of man and his place in the universe.
- The Islamic educational institutions had their own curriculum and the principles of curriculum centred round the Islamic epistemology and axiology which were based on Qur'an and Hadith.
- The Islamic system of education had followed from its very inception the scientific methods like observation, generalization, discussions, debates, sermons, memorization, activity orientation, pragmatic approach etc. which later influenced the educational philosophy of the West.
- In the system of Islamic education, there was constant and regular personal interaction between teachers and pupils which helped the character building of the pupils.
- The mosque was the central institution of the Islamic system of education and the educational institutions were managed with the co-operation of the society.
- There were facilities for students' staying in the Islamic educational institutions. This practice was later adopted by the modern system of education.

- The system of educational management was carried out in the interest of the society based on the principles of Islam.
- It is found that the influence of Islamic philosophy on the Western system of education can be traced in the aims and objectives, curriculum development, curriculum transaction, teacher-pupil interaction and educational management to a certain extent, especially related to the educational ideas of Comenius, Rousseau and John Dewey.
- The comparison in the study revealed that the ideas of the Islamic philosophers who lived before the period of 'Renaissance' had influenced the modern philosophers like Comenius, the father of modern education and Rousseau, the great proponent of freedom in education.
- The cardinal ideas of Islamic Philosophy has been reflected in John Dewey's ideas on education. That is whatever theorized or preached should be put into practice. Moreover Dewey strongly recommended the scientific methods of observation and experimentation in his theories, which had been put forward by the Medieval thinkers like Ibn Sina and Ibn Rushd.
- It can be stated that John Dewey, who received the ideas from the 'Renaissance' writers who followed the Arab scholars, had been indirectly influenced, to a certain extent by the Muslim scholars.

Suggestions for Further Study

The present study attempted to find out the influences of Islamic philosophy on modern educational philosophy. The study has been carried out within a frame work of limited extent. So the findings reported in this study point to the need for further research in the subject. Some areas, as related to the present topic for further research studies are to be carried out, are listed below:

- A separate study can be carried out on the educational contributions of Muslim Spain and its influence on Western Europe.
- A detailed study can be made on the educational systems and educational management during the early Islamic periods.
- A detailed study is to be conducted on the importance of knowledge and education as envisaged in the Holy Qur'an and in the Teachings of Prophet Muhammed.
- An investigation may be done in detail to the Qur'anic instructions of learning by observation of the 'Natural Phenomena'.
- A comparative study can be conducted on the compilation of 'Reason' and 'Revelation' with reference to education.
- The extend of influence exerted in each area and in each philosopher or educationist, by the thoughts of 'Middle Ages', can be done separately.

- A study on the influence of Islamic thoughts on the educational thought of the select European educationalists of 17th and 18th centuries can be made.
- A comparative study of the curricula of the Arab countries and the British National curriculum and curricula in the federal States in the United States of America can be carried out with a view to assessing their mutual influence.
- The influence of Islamic thought on the curricula of the select modern Muslim country can be carried out.
- A study of the influence of modern education on the Islamic education of modern times can be carried out.

The present study has made the investigator to arrive at the conclusion that Islamic philosophy has, to a large extent, influenced the evolution of the Western educational thought and the system of education evolved from it since Renaissance. Its impact on the aspects of the educational ideas and practices of education has been highlighted in the present study, especially when a comparison of thoughts of three eminent Islamic philosophers who lived before Renaissance were made with the educational thoughts of three select modern educational philosophers. However, substantiation of these hypotheses doesn't anyway deny the fact that in turn modern educational philosophy has influenced the Islamic education of modern times which is to be investigated into.

CPSIA information can be obtained
at www.ICGtesting.com
Printed in the USA
LVHW021637120423
744200LV00009B/245

9 784634 992047